Crafting a National Security Strategy for India

Centre for Security Studies

The field of Security Studies is vast and robust, situated within an ever-changing geopolitical and strategic landscape, where new dimensions are being added to the arena every day. At the Centre for Security Studies (CSS), we believe that the various factors and aspects influencing security must be better understood to fully and fairly gauge and examine their effect on contemporary international politics and security. CSS takes a unique, multidisciplinary approach to understanding and analysing security-related issues through in-depth analysis, reports, and policy briefs, which explore regional and thematic topics in the broader field of International Security Studies. Moreover, as the fields of International Relations and International Security have largely been western dominated disciplines, CSS aims to introduce newer perspectives from the Global South to the problems of security. Through this, we work towards aiding intellectuals and policymakers in their task of formulating more comprehensive security policies and strategies that are rooted in a deeper understanding of global dynamics.

The Centre for Security Studies is a student led research Centre, under the aegis of Jindal School of International Affairs, at O.P Jindal Global University.

CSS Security Series 2

Crafting a National Security Strategy for India

Pankaj K Jha
Zeus Hans Mendez
Swati Lakshmi Batchu
Rayan V Bhagwagar

SHIPRA

₹ 995
US$ 40
ISBN: 978-93-88691-78-9

First Published in India in 2021

Crafting a National Security Strategy for India

Published by:
SHIPRA PUBLICATIONS
LG 18-19, Pankaj Central Market
I.P. Ext., Patparganj, Delhi 110092, India
Tel.: +91 11 2223 5152/6152
E-mail: info@shiprapublication.com
www.shiprapublication.com

Contents

Introduction

In an increasingly competitive strategic environment, India has now been positioned as an emerging power, with the potential to become a net security provider in the Indian Ocean region. In this context, it has become imperative that the government of India addresses both security challenges, and scouts for opportunities in a comprehensive manner. It is important to build capabilities which can address any threats to national security. India's growing interconnectedness in the world, clubbed with its positioning as the focal point of South Asia and the Indian Ocean, results in the need for the country to establish itself firmly in geopolitical dynamics. Great power struggle for dominance in the Indo-Pacific, challenges of terrorism and religious radicalization, and military threats from India's neighbours in the North and the West, need to be taken into cognisance. The lens through which these strategic policy initiatives are viewed, will inherently determine both obstacles to India's security infrastructure as well as the course of India's rise as a global power.

In pursuit of this larger goal, there is a need to outline the path that India will adopt. There are no significant official strategic outlines through which one may approach and navigate both internal as well as external security dynamics with the exception of annual reports of MEA and MOD as well as few strategy papers by the defence forces. In this regard, short term planning seemingly still plagues India's security objectives. If the country's strategic and security aspirations are to be enforced, bolstered and achieved, there is a need to address ground realities, shortfalls, threats and challenges across the board. This would mean the outlining of a strategy that is multi-sectoral, and prepares for capability planning and identifying challenges. An establishment of such a framework can contribute towards a concrete and comprehensive national security strategy which highlights weakness and amplifies strengths, while simultaneously addressing internal security threats and protecting strategic autonomy.

In terms of India's internal security, the government still faces numerous old and new challenges as well. While insurgencies and instability haven't been completely quelled in regions like the North East and Naxal affected areas, Daesh (ISIS) returnees and other radicalized individuals pose the threat of perpetuating extremist ideologies that can possibly serve to radicalize others. With proper strategies and adherence to certain norms and recommendations, such internal security challenges can possibly be reduced if not mitigated. At the crux of the proposals lies emphasis on deradicalization and anti-radicalization vis a vis counter radicalization measure. While the latter is undoubtedly essential, it has not and shall not be enough to ensure that India's internal security requirements are met. Additionally, though, the role, purpose, shortfalls and management of security personnel, whether paramilitary or police need to be addressed. This is perhaps best indicative of the fact that tackling India's security challenges requires a coordinated and comprehensive approach. Such an approach will account for multiple objectives, aspirations, capabilities, and organisational deficits, while simultaneously developing a multi-sectoral unified approach and strategy.

On the strategic front, India has been placed at a significant crossroads. For years, it has maintained neutrality (also known as strategic autonomy) in its relationships across the board, especially with regards to China, Russia and the US. However, with increased competition in South Asia, as well as direct threats to India's borders from such neighbours, it is perhaps time for India to outline China as the strategic threat that it is. With recent incursions in Galwan, possible unfair demands in Arunachal (including those related to Tawang) and future threats on India's maritime frontiers, there is a need for India to clearly outline the threats that it faces, whether they be covert or overt. Threats to India security in this regard do not only emanate from traditional mediums, but the use of psychological and information warfare has also become a stark reality. To this end, futuristic planning is required. These are concepts that are increasingly seen in the context of China and must be addressed at the earliest.

Essentially, such challenges, among others can only be addressed through a comprehensive and multisectoral approach as mentioned above. Not only is there a need for India to clearly outline its current defence capabilities, but also ensure that objectives of military modernization and smart forces are achieved. While this will thus increase and improve India's defence security infrastructure, there is also a need to address India's non-traditional security challenges more effectively. India does not only need to develop sophisticated intelligence networks and mechanisms, but also needs to secure its cyber space from threats that are increasing daily. The ideal approach must include the creation of narratives and counter-narratives, along with regulatory and monitoring mechanisms. While it has become increasingly apparent that the challenges that India will face in the coming future are numerous, they are not insurmountable. The only obstacle in achieving success is the lack of coherence in its national security initiatives and frameworks.

In this regard, there are four key arenas that this study shall seek to provide concrete analysis and recommendations on. These are:

1. Highlighting defence capabilities and planning, while simultaneously addressing shortfalls in military modernization, defence procurement and force management.
2. Identifying threats to India's internal security, with a focus on radicalization and stability, while also prescribing strategies that can be adopted in lieu of the same.
3. Navigating India's strategic autonomy during an era of both enhanced cooperation and conflict in its external environment, while prescribing a need for non-neutrality in certain cases.
4. Addressing non-traditional security threats by outlining challenges in both cyber and space while emphasizing the need for upgradation in India's intelligence networks and actionable intelligence collection mechanisms.

The objectives of the study are premised on the need for the Indian security establishment to adopt a unified strategy or at least a coherent and unified approach, that can be disseminated across sectors, ensuring that common goals and objectives are reached and maintained. At the crux of this argument lies the fact that India today lacks coherence in ensuring its security goals are met. This is an objective that is seemingly obscure and ambiguous in nature, and is also possibly an impossibility in the eyes of some. However, the institution of high-level intra-ministry and intra-organizational dialogue and the enforced cooperation of lower-level forces and institutions can seek to bridge gaps that currently prove to be shortfalls in India's security requirements and aspirations; a fact that this study will address.

1

Analysing Security Strategy Documents

An extensive range of reviews, documents, and reports that are critical to understanding the Indian government's progress on issues of national security are created on a near annual basis. These include annual reports of the Ministry of Defence, the Ministry of External Affairs, Ministry of Home Affairs, past special reports, and defence reviews by appointed panels and committees that touch on issues that impact India's national security. These issues range from India's regional and international ties and internal security issues to controlling narcotics trafficking and disaster management. Yet, while these and a plethora of other topics are covered at length, several gaps remain in India's approach to such documents.

There is only ever a cursory mention of India's understanding of the international environment, its place in it, and how it wishes to shape it, in addition to details on current and past priorities. There are significant advantages to presenting such information. Strategic documents are some of the most direct expressions of a state's values, intents, and means. When used tactfully, they can become an important source for not only other states but also non-state or civil society actors to understand and better formulate policy direction. This section will delve into some of these documents to identify gaps in how they envision and present India's national security challenges. It will also consider if India could draw inspiration from other major powers that produce strategic documents that are often broader in scope and provide blueprint for future planning.

Aside from reports by some specially appointed panels, such as the 2001 report by the Group of Ministers, annual reviews and reports by concerned ministries tend to follow a predictable format. Reports are organized according to key issue areas and overwhelming space is used to report on the government activities during the previous year or previous few years. This extensive list of the government's activities certainly has its uses. For one, it keeps ministries accountable to their work. However, these efforts must be equally balanced by a larger review of the effectiveness of these activities, how to correct for issues in programming, and a consideration of what each organization plans for its future and how it aims to achieve it. Such a National Security Strategy document will be a significant step towards reducing the ad hocism that very often plague the operations of India's defence sector. Yet, such activities form a minute part of such documents. Over the years, other than the 2001 report by the Group of Ministers, the report of the Kargil Review Committee, the Report of the Naresh Chandra Task Force on Security (2012), and a document on "Building Comprehensive National Power: Towards an Integrated National Security Strategy" have been created by the Indian government. However, other than the Kargil Review Committee's and the GoM's report, no other documents in the list mentioned above have been made public.

For instance, the Ministry of Home Affair's latest annual report[1] features a detailed listing of the ministry's activities; yet the report does not outline the agency's future plans, nor has the ministry elaborated on areas of improvement. A fairly long section that is dedicated to the ministry's activities to promote cyber security doesn't highlight key gaps in India's cyber security infrastructure. To that point this report will go on to illustrate what these gaps are in a later section. The Ministry of Defence's report[2] does comparatively better, dedicating a few paragraphs to outlining the larger vision guiding defence policies and activities, outlining major challenges, and highlighting measures of decentralization and reform in addition to providing information of the ministry's activities in the previous year. However, these analyses are not common across the spectrum. If it is to be argued that more thorough reviews are best left to panels that look for gaps in the existing security infrastructure, then such reviews and reports must be presented more frequently and consistently.

One such extensive report was that of the Group of Minister's in 2001. The GoM were to review India's security system and the Kargil Review Committee's recommendations. The report is one of the few attempts by the Indian government to conduct a detailed scrutiny of its security apparatus and highlights crucial accomplishments, focus areas, and places for improvement. Crucially, it also highlights the changing strategic environment nationally and internationally and acknowledges the need for a change in future strategy as well as measures to account for this[3]. It also provides detailed recommendations on changes to be made. Since the evaluation of the GoM in 2001, the changes in the security environment predicted have only become more apparent and urgent. Yet, the Indian government's response to them has been slow to materialize. This is not to say the report's recommendations have been ignored in their entirely. The Indian government has gradually improved Indo-US ties since the report's observation of the U.S.' pre-eminence in the global order. It has also adopted the GoM's recommendation to appoint a Chief of Defence Staff (CDS) to further streamline decision making between the armed forces.

Nonetheless, several other critical recommendations regarding formulating better policies for resource procurement, improved defence planning and budgeting, gaining technological advancements to support information warfare, connectivity, etc., have not sufficiently materialized. For instance, there have been several delays in putting out a comprehensive strategy around augmenting cyber and space warfare capabilities, defence modernization, and procurement of critical technologies. The National Cyber Security Strategy is yet to materialize, the first draft of a national space policy was only recently released, and there seems to be little indication of a comprehensive National Security Strategy document being released any time soon. Given that in the past national security documents have been kept classified, it be ensured that any new national security strategy document is made accessible to the public. This will generate public support for defence modernisation plans and also engage the political brass in better financial allocation of defence resources without interfering in the functioning of the armed forces.

The administrative delays caused by repeated lockdowns and the restrictions of working out of office pose one reason for this. Beyond this, however, the absence of any central body coordinating the state's plethora of agencies dedicated to maintaining cyber security and space policy, let alone larger national security plans have made the creation of comprehensive and all-encompassing reviews and strategy documents difficult to achieve. With the creation of a Defence Cyber and a Defence Space Agency, there might be enough stimulus to push such initiatives through. This, of course, would also depend on the coordinating agency's ability to elicit cooperation from actors in various ministries of the government as well.

Had centralization happened early on, perhaps India too could be better positioned to conduct more productive reviews that focus on refining future strategies and capabilities, rather than dwelling on current ones. One example of such a forward-looking document is that of the US National Cyber Strategy. The document adopts the four pillars of America's national security strategy from the country's National Security Strategy Documents and considers its status and future goals for cyber security within the context of these pillars. The pillars are the protection of the American people and the American way of life, to promote American prosperity, to preserve peace through strength, and to advance American interests[4]. For instance, the document highlights the salience of preserving the American way of life and highlights some major actors and issue areas that serve as an obstacle to the successful achievement of this pillar. This is followed up by a breakdown of key national security threats that compromise the safety of the American people and American territory. Here the focus is not on considering past government measures, but to instead look into the future in order to anticipate what security threats will be the most salient for the United States.

This component of long-term planning and a cohesive multi-sectoral national security strategy that encompasses both domestic and international threats, and takes multiple bodies of the government into consideration simultaneously is absent in any Indian documents. The closest any official agency document has gotten to achieving this, other than the Ministry of Defence, is the Ministry of External Affairs' short outline of India's national interests followed by the mention of diplomatic measures that aim to cater to these interests[5]. However, this is as far as any of the major agencies got to explicitly providing significant context to ongoing national security issues. Here too, MEA failed to project how current and future threats formulate into the kind of security and diplomatic architecture India wishes to have nationally, regionally, and internationally.

This isn't the only area where India could borrow lessons from other major powers. Issues with the lack of an overall strategic framework translate onto other key subjects as well, such as defence capability planning. India has not yet produced a comprehensive defence capability plan, instead creating multiple individual reports on topics of defence procurement, a technology roadmap, cyber security, etc. The MoD has been fairly successful in creating and regularly modifying its Defence Acquisition Procedure (DAP)[6] to respond to new challenges with procurement as they appear. In this sense the DAP, although it is only a procedural guide, has been quite adaptive. Other major powers, such as Australia, employ the use of a Force Structure Plan[7] in addition to issuing specific documents to outline its current and future investments into the nation's defence force. This integrated plan outlines the range of capabilities the Australian armed forces possess not only in the domains of land, sea, and air, but also in terms of strategic partnerships and technological advancements.

Moreover, such observations and future plans are contextualized within the state's goals to actively shape its immediate environment to suit its strategic needs and deter any security threats. Through this structure, the Australian government provides a holistic review of its armed force's current capacities and presents the trajectory the government and the armed forces will take in the future to ensure that such capacity continues to develop in support of the country's geo-strategic goals. Given that India not only lacks the larger strategic framework, but also lacks a consolidated analysis of the security apparatus's capabilities across forces and agencies, such a goal is not currently achievable. This can prove to be a hurdle in formulating a cohesive plan for weapons procurement, technology transfer, military modernization and more across the board as will be amply shown.

The final difference to be pointed out here is the language utilized in the report. This refers to the tone and connotation of the writing. These elements can reveal much about a state's strategic thinking and choices. For instance, major international and regional powers are increasingly leaning towards explicitly naming their allies and rivals in strategic documents as threat perception increases. This was the case with Australia as it named China as a significant player in the Indo-Pacific where it sees rising instability manifesting in its defence strategy plan. While not singularly naming and blaming China, associating China's status in the Indo-Pacific and rising tensions in the region within the context of the harsh rhetoric coming from Canberra, one can quickly surmise Australia's changing position on China's role in the high seas. The United States is even more explicit in its retort of China's economic and political policies given their rivalry.

This can help countries attract partners that are more in tune with their national goals. India could thus benefit from it as well. A vague stance may allow the state more room to manoeuvre internationally politically and diplomatically, but it can also create hesitation with partners who wish to form strong partnerships along with clear objectives. Thus, it might be to India's benefit to similarly identify its key rivals in terms of its political and strategic situation. However, India's strongest rival, China, relies on masking its strategic goals and does not name its key enemies in its strategic documents to maintain a perception of neutrality internationally. This has helped them expand their influence within the developing world. Thus, while there are benefits to stating a clear position in its national strategy, India must be mindful of China's approach and strategy and find approaches to counter them in its own strategy.

Notes

1. Ministry of Home Affairs. (2019). Annual Report. Retrieved from: https://www.mha.gov.in/sites/default/files/AnnualReport_English_01102019.pdf
2. Ministry of Defence (2019). Annual Report. Retrieved from: https://www.mod.gov.in/sites/default/files/MoDAR2018.pdf
3. Government of India. (2001). Report of the Group of Ministers on National Security. Chapter 1. Retrieved from: https://www.vifindia.org/sites/default/files/GoM%20Report%20on%20National%20Security.pdf
4. White House. (2018, December). National Security Strategy. Retrieved from: https://www.whitehouse.gov/wp-content/uploads/2018/09/National-Cyber-Strategy.pdf
5. Ministry of External Affairs. (2020). Annual Report. Retrieved from: http://www.mea.gov.in/Uploads/PublicationDocs/32489_AR_Spread_2020_new.pdf
6. Ministry of Defence. (2020). Defence Acquisition Procedure. Retrieved from: https://www.mod.gov.in/dod/sites/default/files/DAP2030new_0.pdf
7. Department of Defense. (2020). Force Structure Plan. Retrieved from Department of Defense, Government of Australia: https://www1.defence.gov.au/sites/default/files/2020-11/2020_Force_Structure_Plan.pdf

2

India's Strategic Environment

For centuries, India was the at centre of a massive network of trade and communication that spanned the Indian Ocean; a dynamic that was never emphasized upon enough during the formative years of the country's strategic policy. Today, India does not only lie within a complex geo-strategic environment, but also within a constantly evolving one. There is therefore a need for India to chalk out a clear path in ensuring self-sustenance, strategic prowess, force projection and simultaneous strategic autonomy in its neighbourhood and beyond. With a growing strategic presence, expanding economy and increasing global importance, India must ensure that its strategic objectives are met; especially in lieu of the growing threats that it faces. Across its north, east, and western frontiers, India is faced by the growing assertiveness of China on the one hand, and increasing border tensions and incursions on the other; while on the seas, stakeholders as well as security threats have increased across the Indian Ocean. In this regard, India has been placed at a point in time, where it requires an increase in both, its domestic prowess as well as its international collaborations.

On the latter, India has built on a number of crucial relations over the years, upgrading many bilateral relationships to the status of strategic partnerships. India's growing economy, geostrategic location and mix of diplomatic foreign policy has ensured ties with countries across the globe. Countries considered the closest to India today, include the United States, the Russian Federation, Japan, France, and Israel among others. Additionally, though, India has forged a number of other strategic relationships with others including Oman, Singapore, South Africa, Brazil, Vietnam, Indonesia, etc. The detailing of a few of these relationships, which are not only increasingly crucial to India today, but also which can be built on further have been highlighted below.

India's Strategic and Congenial partners

The United States

The Indian-US bilateral relationship is slowly being transformed into a strong strategic partnership. Regular exchanges through high-level political visits have provided for and sustained the momentum between the two largest democracies of the world. Today this partnership is broad based and multi-sectoral, covering trade, logistics, security and defence, high-technology, civil-nuclear energy, space technology and cyber security. The defence and strategic relationship has emerged as a major pillar in the US-India partnership, at the crux of which lies the need to counter Chinese influence in the region and simultaneously bolster US presence in Asia.

Over the past one and half decades, the relationship between India and the US has improved substantially, beginning with an agreement on civil nuclear energy cooperation in 2005 and culminating in the signing of the final foundational security agreement in 2020. Along with cooperation and regular defence procurement, India has also conducted a number of joint exercises and drills in the Indian Ocean. Today, possible collaboration across the Blue Dot Network and cooperation in the Quadrilateral Security Dialogue has reinforced the partnership. In 2018, the first ever 2+2 dialogue was held with the US among joint exercises such as Cope-India (Air Force), Yudh Abhyas (Army) and Vajra Prahar (Special Forces). The two sides are also increasingly engaged in a number of multilateral exercises such as the MALABAR, RED FLAG and RIMPAC exercises.

The first 2+2 dialogue has been followed by two others in 2019 and 2020. These dialogues have been symbolic due to the fact that they have established key logistics agreements with the United States; among other factors. The dialogue saw India and the US conclude a number of agreements including, the Industrial Security Annex, a Coalition for Disaster Resilient Infrastructure (CDRI), Finalisation of the Defence Technology and Trade Initiative (DTTI), a new Science and Technology Agreement (S&T), Space Situational Awareness agreement, as well as expansion of cooperation under the Indo-Pacific Initiative.[1] In accordance with the ever-enhancing ties though, over the course of the past few years, in bolstering the strategic partnership, the Logistics Memorandum Agreement, the Communications Compatibility and Security Agreement and the Basic Exchange and Cooperation Agreement have been signed. These agreements have sought to establish a degree of interoperability between the two militaries; a definitive boost to the security partnership.

1. **General Security of Military Information Agreement (GSOMIA)** - The General Security of Military Information Agreement was signed in 2002 to provide a framework for exchange and protection of classified military information between the US and Indian defence sectors and became the first comprehensive information sharing agreement between the US and India. The agreement was bolstered in 2019 with the signing of the Industrial Security Annex (ISA) which eased the transfer of high-level technology between US and Indian defence manufacturers and industries.[2]
2. **Cyber MOU** - In 2011, the United States and India signed a Memorandum of Understanding aimed at promoting closer cooperation and timely exchange of information between organizations and ministries of both governments with regards to cybersecurity and cyber related risks. The MOU established best practices for the exchange of critical cybersecurity information and expertise between the two governments; primarily through the Indian Computer Emergency Response Team (CERT-In), Department of Information Technology, Ministry of Communications and Information Technology, and DHS' United States Computer Emergency Readiness Team (US-CERT).
3. **LEMOA** - The Logistics Exchange memorandum of Agreement, which is an India-specific version of the Logistics Support Agreement was signed in 2016. This agreement gives access to both countries to designate military facilities on either side for the purpose of refuelling, replenishment, etc. The LEMOA essentially ensures cooperation in port calls, resource sharing, maintenance services, joint exercises, joint training, humanitarian assistance and disaster relief. The LEMOA agreement was fully operationalised in 2018.
4. **COMCASA** - The Communications Compatibility and Security Agreement was signed in 2018 and aimed at enhancing communications sharing on the defence platforms of either country. Not only will the COMCASA allow India access to more advanced communications technology for defence equipment purchased from the US, but also increase the interoperability and coordination of Indian, US and US allied forces in real time. Essentially, the agreement will also pave the way for the fitting of special communications systems on Indian platforms like the C 130J and the Naval P 8I aircraft that will allow them to interact with the US military. It will also possibly give India access to advanced new defence systems like armed drones and allow the Indian armed forces to exploit existing US-origin platforms more efficiently. The signing of the COMCASA was also accompanied by the initiation of other mechanisms aimed at cooperation between the US and India. The 2+2 dialogue

launched a new "tri-services exercise" called Tiger Triumph and a new agreement on defence innovation as well as reaffirmed existing areas of agreement on counterterrorism and cybersecurity.

5. **BECA** - The latest and final agreement in the three foundational agreements to be signed between the United States and India is the Basic Exchange and Cooperation Agreement. Signed in October 2020 between the National Geospatial-Intelligence Agency of the US Department of Defense and India's Ministry of Defence, the agreement allows both countries to share essential military information on geospatial data. These include the sharing of geomagnetic and gravity data, maps, nautical and aeronautical charts, commercial and other unclassified imagery. The key reasoning for this agreement is the need to ensure greater accuracy of Indian missiles and armed drones that need such data.

For a long time, there has been debate over the extent to which the Indian administration must align with the US and its strategic objectives. With respect to shared interests, India and the United States share an interest in promoting a rule based international order while simultaneously preventing Chinese hegemony in Asia. Ultimately though, it is speculated that India would prefer a multipolar Asia rather than one that perpetuates US primacy. It has however become apparent it is only after making calculated assessments of India's strategic environment, that the government has decided in recent years to bolster its partnership with the US. The three agreements (COMCASA, LEMOA and BECA) are considered foundational pacts or agreements that the US signs with any of the countries it seeks to enhance its security partnership with. The United States has similar agreements with its NATO partners and other treaty partners like Japan and the Philippines. While each agreement in and of itself merely signifies a step towards greater collaboration between the two countries, but taken together they signify a significant shift in Indian foreign policy and strategic thinking.

It must be noted however, that while a sophisticated engagement with the US is in India's interests, it must not contribute towards a self-perception of defeatism; an assumption that the US will become a crutch against China. India must essentially remain wary of the concessions, if any, that the United States will be willing to make through these agreements, so as not to give more than it receives. The alteration of the original names of the Logistics Support Arrangement (LSA) to the LEMOA and the Communication and Information on Security Memorandum of Agreement (CISMOA) to the COMCASA have been seen as ensuring Indian autonomy; allowing it to enter into an arrangement of convenience, rather than an alliance. While this is seemingly true, it must not become a mere fig leaf that can be leveraged to the US' benefit. With all three agreements currently signed and adopted, the Indian government must maintain a sense of superiority over its own autonomy in the operability of its armed forces and its foreign policy objectives; especially in lieu of maintaining its relationship with Russia.

Logistical issues also include the adoption of certain standard operating procedures, and financing procedures that may not be suitable for enhanced cooperation between all three wings of the Indian Armed Forces. This however, is set to change and could become a beneficial tool for India to increase the coordination of its own armed forces. If used, negotiated and operated accordingly, these security engagements would provide the Indian government with key benefits; including aid in the rescue of stranded Indians in conflict or disaster zones; enhance the military capabilities of India to protect its strategic influence and interests in the Indo-Pacific; enhance coordination with the US military in the event of an actual conflict.

Yet, what the relationship now requires is a bolstering of cooperation in a number of arenas. India must firstly tap into the larger multilateral architecture that the United States fosters for its security engagements, a fact that is already occurring, yet needs enhancement. Secondly, while agreements of interoperability and defence exercises have been initiated, this must be facilitated in other sectors as well, including more combined operations, higher technological cooperation and intelligence cooperation. There essentially remains to be an institutionalization of intelligence cooperation, a fact that must be reviewed.

Nonetheless, the agreements and other steps taken in bolstering the Indo-US strategic partnership are a clear indication of the steps India is willing to take in ensuring its own security along with stability in its neighbourhood. The key goal in this regard, is in countering Chinese aggression. Building on ties with the United States through a constructive approach which is friendly, yet maintains its neutrality, would inevitably achieve the above stated goals. In this, the Government of India must be cautious of US influence in the region, yet utilise its presence and the resources it is granted through this strategic partnership to its full.

Russia

Since the signing of the Declaration on the India-Russia Strategic Partnership in October 2000, India-Russia collaboration has been enhanced and broadened across sectors, including science, defence, security, trade and technology. Yet as mentioned above, the primary focus of the same lies on defence and security. These are largely facilitated by a number of institutionalised dialogue mechanisms operating across political and official levels. On the defence and security front, the relationship has evolved from one based on mere defence transactions to one involving joint research, development and production of advanced defence technologies and systems. The BrahMos Missile System as well as the licensed production of the SU-30 aircraft and the T-90 tanks are indicative of this.

Recent bilateral initiatives have included an agreement on cooperation in the production of spare parts for Russian military equipment in September 2019, agreements on the supply of S-400 air defence systems, the construction of frigates under Project 11356 and on the joint venture to manufacture Ka-226T helicopter in India. A recent joint initiative aimed at the production of the AK Series Assault Rifles was also announced in 2019. India and Russia also launched their first ever Tri-Services exercise called the INDRA, which took place in Vladivostok in 2017 and was then followed by another one in Pune and Goa in 2019.

India's strategic relationship also continues to be premised on defence transactions, the most recent of which has been the purchase of 33 Russian fighter jets, including 21 MiG-29 and 12 Su-30 MKI. The recent purchase, worth a total of $2.4 billion also included provisions for the upgrades of 59 existing MiG-29s. The Russian government has recently also fulfilled India's defence requirement earlier than expected, in lieu of the increased tensions across the Galwan border with China. Such initiatives are indicative of the fact that the relationship between India and Russia remains strong, whether in terms of actual cooperation or realpolitik.

While strategists and policy analysts have held for a while that India-Russian ties will become distanced in lieu of increased cooperation with the United States, this is not wholly true. Rifts are possible in the coming future, but the relationship, which is officially labelled as a "special and privileged strategic partnership", is set to endure. What one must note is that Russia has been a dependable partner on most strategic standpoints with India; even more so than the United States. The Trump administration had shown increased support for India, however, there are still many US congressmen and women who are highly critical of India on numerous issues. A change in administration will now signify a change in attitude towards India. While a Biden administration would undoubtedly continue the high-level engagements with India, it could possibly also be more critical in other matters. These are issues that the relationship with Russia lacks. Russia reserves its comments on India's internal issues while simultaneously continuing cooperation across sectors.

Finally, bolstering the bilateral partnership, allows for increased autonomy in foreign policy strategic objectives of both countries; especially since neither India nor Russia are set to become junior partners to either China or the United States. Today, the relationship may not be as robust or as comprehensive as it once was, but both countries have continued regular defence transactions and exercises; with the latest being held in September 2020. Such provisions allow for India to exercise its strategic autonomy and navigate between stronger powers; while simultaneously building on both old and new partnerships that it requires.

France

The signing of the strategic partnership in 1998 established a relationship between India and France that would grow to encompass cooperation across nuclear, space, defence, cyber security, intelligence sharing and counter terrorism. In December 2019, France announced that it would conduct joint patrols in the southern and north western Indian Ocean; a development that was indicative of a certain divergence from the Indian policy of only executing Coordinated Patrols (CORPAT) with its essential neighbours. This has been preceded by a series of agreements, joint statements, and MoUs between the two countries, starting with the release of the Joint Strategic Vision of India-France Cooperation in the Indian Ocean Region, launched by Prime Minister Modi and President Macron in 2018.[3] Under this initiative, India and France would work to integrate their coastal radar stations across the region with countries like Mauritius, Seychelles and Madagascar; countries in which India has already installed radars and other critical technical networks.

The bilateral discussions during the same meeting were largely focused on defence, maritime, space, security, and energy-related sectors, and also explored the possibilities of research on high tech Nano satellites, thermal imaging and night vision devices, high tech radars, underwater UAVs and mine countermeasures at sea. Since then, though, the relationship has only been bolstered further. The institution of the ministerial-level Annual Defence Dialogue in 2018, which was replicated in 2019 has also been established as a regular feature in the Indo-French strategic dynamic. Additionally, regular bilateral military exercises between the three services beginning with the navies in 2001 (VARUNA), the air forces in 2005 (GARUDA) and armies in 2011 (SHAKTI) have also become essential in this regard.

India and France have also begun conducting coordinated maritime surveillance patrols in the Indian Ocean, the latest of which was held in late March 2020. The patrol was conducted by a P-81 aircraft with French Navy personnel onboard in a clear break from the past, elevating cooperation and collaboration.[4] These surveillance sorties have now been touted as a regular feature in the Indo-French strategic cooperation in the Indian Ocean. There is therefore a definitive stance being adopted by the Indian government in increasing both cooperation and possible interoperability with a number of foreign countries in the Indian Ocean; France being a key factor in the same.

With regards to possible interoperability between the Armed Forces of India and France, an agreement for the provision of Reciprocal Logistics Support was also signed in 2018. The agreement, which has been operationalised in 2019, will facilitate the French and Indian armed forces to receive logistical support, supplies and services from each other during authorised port visits, joint training, joint exercise, humanitarian assistance and disaster relief. Such agreements and cooperation have also coincided with joint defence related projects; the main of which is the purchase of the Rafale aircraft and the P-75 Scorpene Project.

1. **Purchase of Rafale** - The agreement for the purchase of 36 Rafale jets by India in flyaway condition was signed on 23 September 2016 and is currently underway. The first of the fighter aircrafts were handed over on the 8th of October at Bordeaux and the first batch reached India in July 2020. The delivery is set to be completed by the end of 2021.
2. **P-75 Scorpene Project** - The contract for six Scorpene submarines from M/s DCNS (now Naval Group) was signed in October of 2006. All the vessels are to be built under technology transfer at the Mazagon Docks Ltd., and the project is well underway. The first submarine, the INS Kalvari was commissioned in December 2017.

The relationship between India and France is largely motivated by France's stake in the region. This stake exists in the presence of the overseas French territories of the Islands of La Reunion, Myotte and French Southern and Antarctic Territories; as well as Cliperton, French Polynesia, New Caledonia and the Wallis and Futuna Islands across the Indo-Pacific. These territories provide France with one of the largest Exclusive Economic Zones in the world which is over 10 million square kilometres in area. In this regard, France has in fact sought to build useful links and joint actions in the name of shared security, as underscored at the Shangri-La dialogue in 2019 by French Minister of the Armed Forces, Florence Parly.

French presence in the Indo-Pacific however, is critical in providing for India's security challenges in a constantly evolving strategic environment. Firstly, both India and France have a shared commitment to ensuring the freedom of navigation, maintaining a fight against maritime piracy, and also increasing cooperation in both climate related and economic sectors. Secondly though, both India and France benefit greatly from an enhanced bilateral security partnership. While closer relations with India and increased engagements in the Indian Ocean pave the way for greater French engagement with both South and Southeast Asian countries, India also benefits greatly from a partnership which is based on shared ideals of multilateralism, pluralism and deterrence-based policy.

Basing a security partnership on mere ideals however does not always bode well for security, and therefore it is time for the Indian government to utilize and leverage this partnership better. This is especially vital as a relationship with France is unburdened by the domestic political pressures that come into play with other relationships, as French support for India has had a bipartisan consensus since the establishment of the Strategic Partnership in 1998[5]. The possibility of this reality soon being leveraged is however also becoming apparent, with the number of agreements, defence procurements, visits and exercises that have now been regularised between the two nations.

France does not only have the potential of becoming an integral element in India's security framework for the Indian Ocean through cooperation in geospatial intelligence and information sharing, but also possibly in other multilateral forums as well. It recently joined India and Australia in initiating a new trilateral dialogue signalling strategic convergence in the Indo-Pacific region; a definitive indication of shifting priorities and perceptions of China's growing rise. In this regard, it is becoming increasingly apparent that France's priorities in the Indo-Pacific are being realigned in such a way as to provide India with further opportunities as well. Increased cooperation in the India-France strategic partnership has gradually been actualized across sectors, and regular and increased collaboration will only bolster the strategic partnership further.

Japan

The foundation of the India-Japan strategic partnership was consolidated in 2007 when Prime Minister Shinzo Abe of Japan presented his "Confluence of Seas" speech in the Indian Parliament. Abe in his speech stated that "The Pacific and the Indian Oceans are now bringing about a dynamic coupling as seas of freedom and prosperity.... Our two countries have the ability and the responsibility to ensure that it broadens yet further and to nurture and enrich these seas to become seas of clearest transparency." In line with these dynamics, India and Japan have initiated a number of bilateral and multilateral military drills, Joint Working Groups in defence technology and annual Ministerial-level dialogues as well as lower-level diplomatic initiatives.

Japan is essentially the only other country, other than the United States and Australia, with which India has conducted a high level two plus two foreign and defence ministerial format dialogue. While two plus two dialogues have been ongoing since 2010, the 2019 dialogue essentially signified a significant upgrade in the partnership. The dialogue allowed for the two countries to try and finalize the military logistics agreement called the Acquisition and Cross-Servicing Agreement. While the agreement has not yet come to fruition, when it does it will enhance the close military engagement between the two countries allowing India access to Japan's naval facility in Djibouti and Japan access to a few facilities in the Andaman and Nicobar Islands.[6]

In this regard, Japan is also increasingly poised to become a major partner in the Indo-Pacific. Not only is it a key member of the Quadrilateral Security Dialogue (QUAD) along with Australia and the United States, but it has also increased its bilateral engagements with India in the Indo-Pacific. In making pledges to "work together towards a free and open Indo-Pacific region," both India and Japan have continuously emphasized the need to enhance collaborative projects and initiatives in the Indo-pacific. In this, both have recognized the need to accelerate maritime security cooperation and also increase the frequency of bilateral naval exercises in the region. This collaboration has also materialized in partnership and investments in the strategically sensitive Andaman and Nicobar Islands as well, where Japan has not only undertaken a number of development projects, but also been contracted to install an undersea cable from Chennai to the islands.[7] In this regard, collaboration between India and Japan is not wholly based on security and defence, but also on technological cooperation.

In 2018, in building on mutual investments support, collaboration on digital infrastructure and system designs, research and development, India and Japan also inked a digital partnership agreement. The agreement essentially allows for research and development in new technologies, including AI and other critical technologies. In October 2018, in a clear message to China, India and Japan have essentially finalized an agreement that provides for cooperation in 5G technology and artificial intelligence. Much of this collaboration is motivated by the need to constrain a number of Chinese telecommunication initiatives that are increasingly being seen as strategic threats by countries across the globe. In this, Japan has also agreed to be the lead partner in the Indo-Pacific Ocean's Initiative (IPOI); the India-backed framework aimed at expanding and facilitating regional cooperation of India's maritime neighbours.

In this regard, India and Japan have also partaken in a number of multilateral initiatives in the regions. While collaboration with the QUAD continues, leaders at the two-plus-two dialogue in 2019 also reaffirmed their support for the ASEAN Outlook on the Indo-Pacific (AOIP) adopted at the 34th Summit in Bangkok in 2019. In this, both India and Japan have noted that India's "Indo-Pacific Oceans Initiative," and Japan's "Vientiane Vision 2.0," have overlapping objectives and interests with the ASEAN's AOIP initiative. Additionally, both countries have cooperated in a number of joint projects in other IOR countries. A key project in this regard is the joint project being initiated in building the East Container Terminal at the Port of Colombo.

On the development front, within India, Japan has committed to providing a loan of 4.5 billion USD for the development of the Delhi-Mumbai Economic Corridor and the development of the Dighi Port in Mumbai. It has also invested in a number of other energy and infrastructure projects in India, with a focus on the North East. In this, the Indian government has essentially opened up avenues for cooperation with Japan in a number of sectors, building on mutual objectives and trust in even granting access to strategic regions like the North East and Andaman and Nicobar.

It is thus evident that Indo-Japan ties have been granted renewed opportunities in cooperation across the board. The new government of Prime Minister Yoshihide Suga has also agreed to retain a strong emphasis on strategic ties with India; a fact that the Indian government must also build upon. Enhanced cooperation on the bilateral front essentially means that the emergence of a Sino-centric Asia is forestalled. As highlighted by ex-Prime Minister Shino Abe, Japan and India are natural allies, wherein "A strong India benefits Japan and a strong Japan benefits India." In this regard, convergence between India and Japan demonstrates a need based deepening trust and a matured partnership; dynamics that can offer numerous possibilities in collaboration and cooperation.

Australia

India-Australia ties have finally been elevated above the nascent stage they had stagnated in for decades. With collaboration across sectors, today, all the major elements of a robust defence and security partnership are in place. Australia and India are essentially natural partners in that they are positioned in critical geopolitical locations; defined by the oceans that surround them. In this, their need to cooperate in the Indo-Pacific has come to the forefront. However, Canberra and New Delhi are not only motivated by the need to promote a rules-based order in the Indo-Pacific, but are also now influenced by the growing threat that China has become. For many years, Australia remained a neutral party in most geopolitical matters concerning China; increasingly collaborating with China on trade and other economic fronts. Essentially, until 2016, Australia "welcomed China's growing participation in International forums," and also promised to "expand its defence relationship with China over the coming years."[8] However, with Australia seeing the stability of the Indo-Pacific and its immediate neighbourhood being threatened by China, it has sought to re-emphasize the need for security collaboration with other countries in the Indo-Pacific; laying an emphasis on the Quad and thus with India.

Australia's transformed outlook towards the Indo-Pacific has essentially translated into stronger ties with India. While it's previous defence and strategy papers saw the Indo-Pacific largely as a region for increased cooperation, today Australia perceives this region and its immediate neighbourhood through a lens of competition and conflict. In this, its 2020 Defence Strategic Update essentially states that "Since 2016, major powers have become more assertive in advancing their strategic preferences and seeking to exert influence, including China's active pursuit of greater influence in the Indo-Pacific."[9] Herein, Australia's need to secure its neighbourhood has essentially granted India with the opportunity to increase cooperation with Australia, and created for itself another strategic partnership. This partnership has now been enshrined in the "Comprehensive Strategic Partnership" that India signed with Australia in June 2020.

In acknowledging that the CSP essentially "takes the Indo-Australia bilateral relationship to a new level of cooperation, based on mutual understanding, trust, common interests and the shared values of democracy and the rule of law," both countries have established a strategies two-plus-two dialogue with their Foreign and Defence Ministers.[10] This does not however symbolize the beginning of strategic ties, and the two countries have embarked upon a steadily growing defence partnership since 2000. This partnership now includes close cooperation on Indian Ocean security, high-level strategic dialogues, military exchanges and training, sophisticated bilateral naval exercises, and most recently, a logistics support agreement.

The Quad retains most of the attention on both ties though, and India must look towards possibilities in bilateral collaboration. Nonetheless, Australia's inclusion within the formal structures, forums and activities of the Quad also grants India renewed opportunities and increased countering capabilities against China. In this, Australia has at numerous instances requested to participate in the Malabar naval exercises with the US and Japan, however, it hasn't yet been formally included into the exercise. With the changing geopolitical dynamics though, this may soon become a reality. Both countries have worked together in establishing the Indian Ocean Rim Association secretariat in Mauritius, and also worked closely with Indonesia during its chairmanship of the organization between 2015-2016. In this, it is evident that both India and Australia share a similar outlook towards cooperation and security in the Indo-Pacific and New Delhi must thus build on these norms.

Beyond multilateral collaboration though, Australia and India have increased their own bilateral engagements, with a significant increase in defence exercises, high level meetings and activities from 11 in 2014 to 38 in 2018, and more in 2020.[11] Since 2015, the AUSINDEX, the main bilateral exercise between the two nations has been held every two years. The 2019 edition of the exercise was especially significant with the number of participating vessels and personnel increasing exponentially. Along with four Australian ships, armed forces and a total of more than 1000 Australian personnel, the exercises also included both Indian and Australian P-8 maritime patrol aircrafts, as well as anti-submarine warfare exercises.[12] With booth militaries possessing a growing number of shared platforms in the c-17 strategic transport aircraft, the C-130 tactical aircraft, P-8 maritime reconnaissance aircraft and the Chinook heavy-lift helicopters, their interoperability is only likely to improve.

Both countries have also partaken in third country led exercises including the United States' Rim of the Pacific Exercise (RIMPAC) and the Western Pacific Naval Symposium Multilateral Sea Exercise (WMSX) in the Singapore Strait and South China Sea. Through such exercises it has become increasingly evident that collaboration between the two countries has only increased. These dynamics have recently been mirrored in the signing of the Mutual Logistics Support Agreement (MLSA). This agreement will facilitate reciprocal access to military bases for logistics support, and also establish a foundation for interoperability between the security forces of the two nations.

Finally, it must be acknowledged that India-Australia relations are still constrained by a number of factors. The first is evidently geographical and perspective based. While many in Australian strategic circles have emphasised the weight of the Indo-Pacific in bring India into a broader strategic space, it is unlikely that India will for the near future seek to exert its military prowess beyond the Indian Ocean. For India, the Indian Ocean will take precedence while the southwest Indian Ocean and the South Pacific will remain the priority for Australia; even though Australia would seek for a larger role played by India. The lack of Indian cooperation and strategic collaboration with the United States in the past had constrained Indo-Australia ties for many years as well, with the relationship not fully incorporating integrated signals intelligence, embedded command structures and tactical intelligence sharing during joint exercises.

Nonetheless, with India now increasing its collaboration and cooperation with the US through the COMCASA, LEMOA and other such agreements, benefits will be found in the India-Australia strategic partnership as well. Additionally, China's growing aspirations and assertiveness will further motivate Australia to maintain its strategic ties with India. In this regard, while cooperation between Australia and India in the coming years will undoubtedly increase, constraints may be found in the manner in which this happens. The Indian government needs to thus assess differences in perspectives in the Indo-Pacific and work around these challenges so that it only draws in another security partner, rather than distance it.

Israel

For decades, India has maintained a very cordial relationship with the state of Israel. Initial opposition at the UN transformed into a budding alliance of convenience. Only after the fall of the Soviet Union did both countries begin to embark upon a strategic partnership, with Israel emerging as one of India's most important military suppliers, second only to Russia. Since Prime Minister Modi has come to power in India, there seems to be a very different relationship in the cards, one that has not been seen between the two countries before. Today, through cross-sectoral collaboration, both countries have established a strong and extensive economic, military and strategic partnership. This partnership has expanded to collaboration in not only defence, but also in science and technology, trade, space, agriculture, oil and natural gas agreements.

India's positioning as Israel's largest arms exporter has meant that defence procurement deals have included a number of different weapons and defence procurements. These include the procurement of Unmanned Aerial Vehicles (UAVs) like the Heron-TP and the Searcher UAVs; Air to Air missiles like the Derby and Python-5 AAMs, fire control radars, multifunction radars, Command and Control Air Defence systems and the Long and Medium Range Surface to Air missiles. The Barak 8 and Barak 1 Surface to Air Missiles, which also constitute a joint development program between India and have been developed by the Israel Aerospace Industries (IAI) and the Rafael Advanced Defence systems companies, in conjunction with both the Indian Navy and the Defence Research and Development Organization (DRDO).[13] In this, the government has also overcome certain obstacles in past collaboration by removing certain Israeli defence companies which were blacklisted in 2006 due to kickback accusations.

While India and Israel may be leagues apart in distance, many of the external security challenges the two states face are quite akin to each other. Hostile neighbours and persistent acts of terror by state and not-state actors alike have created a common ground for security and intelligence related collaboration between the two partners for decades. Today the threat of terrorism on the border of either country forms the basis for strategic collaboration between the intelligence agencies. Israel is considered one of the most efficient countries in dealing with border security and management; especially since it has been continuously plagued by both war or infiltration. In this regard, its defence companies offer highly sophisticated border surveillance and security technology and mechanisms, including electronic and virtual fences, with video motion detection capabilities; electro-optical-based surveillance; autonomous unmanned aerial, ground and maritime patrol vehicles;

advanced thermal imagers and long-range radars as well as underground sensors to detect tunnels.

India needs such technologies in a number of areas, including both the Pakistan and the Bangladeshi border; which are prone to infiltrations. In 2016, an elaborate five-year plan was approved for the western border with Pakistan, which would include a smart Israel-developed fencing system having a quick response team mechanism along with CCTV cameras, thermal image and night-vision devices, underground monitoring sensors and laser barriers.[14] It has thus become apparent that collaboration between India and Israel have already reached significant heights especially on border protection. The advanced technological and strategic experience of Israel in managing complex borders makes it a perfect partner for India's smart border management initiatives.

Additionally, India and Israel have increased cooperation in intelligence sharing. Cooperation between the two countries in this regard have existed for decades, however, recent collaboration has shown an increase in agreements. One such agreement, the Agreement on Co-operation in Homeland and Public Security Issues, has formed the basis for many shared counter-terrorism efforts.[15] The agreement allows for intelligence sharing under its gambit and states that are party to the agreement would "cooperate through the use and procurement of knowledge, experience, information, technology, and scientific research". Area of cooperation listed under Article 2 of the agreement explicitly includes "Investigation and intelligence for public security" among a host of other areas.[16] The Agreement on Co-operation on Homeland and Public Security was signed in tandem with the Agreement on the Protection of Classified Material and a later MoU on cybersecurity.[17]

Recently, India and Israel also signed an agreement that would increase and expand cooperation in cyber security. The agreement doesn't only lay down a framework for dialogue, cooperation in capacity building and mutual exchange of best practices in the field, but also expand the scope of exchange of information on cyber threats. Such agreement especially holds value in a time when India has been facing a growing number of security threats and challenges; as it chooses to diversify and facilitate its "Digital India" initiatives.

Essentially, while many other countries have imposed limitations on procurement by India, Israel has sourced much of its defence deals without restriction; thus, gaining the tag of an "all-weather friend" of India. In this regard, this relationship will seemingly be sustained by a few key factors. The first being the personal relationship inculcated by the current Prime Ministers of both countries. The second is the fact that Israel's defence industry is reliant on export for its survival, and India serves as a perfect partner in this regard.

Thirdly, India and Israel have a major need in collaborating in countering terrorism, with India standing to gain greatly from this relationship and the technical expertise that Israel can provide. And finally, collaboration across sectors in trade, tourism, science and technology, and space has effectively meant that today, Indo-Israel ties have been established as sustainable.

Qatar

India has for decades had a strong civilian presence across the states that constitute West Asia. Qatar has not been an exception – with the over-half-million strong Indian community in the country supporting the furtherance of its development and progress. Qatar, along with other West Asian states has in a short span on time gone on to become a global hub for trade and communication. It is one of the several sources of Indian crude oil imports, importing an estimated USD 1.2 billion worth crude oil in the fiscal year 2018-19. Qatar also happens to be India's largest supplier of liquified natural gas. This makes the country an important factor in India's energy equation.

Qatar has also evolved into a key player in the politics of the region with its pursuance of a regionally independent foreign policy. The country has at multiple occasions been at the centre of regional diplomatic events. This may be in way of the Qatari diplomatic crisis of 2017, as well as the long process of Afghan-Taliban Peace Talks, mediated by Doha. Qatar also actively supported the revolutionary movements that were part of the Arab Spring of 2011, providing revolutionaries with funding and weaponry.

In a step to further diversify foreign policy in West Asia, India is pushing for closer cooperation in the sphere of security, both regionally and extra-regionally. In 2008, then Prime Minister of India, Dr Manmohan Singh alongside HE the Emir of Qatar Sheikh Hamad bin Khalifa Al-Thani signed an agreement on cooperation in security and law enforcement matters. Per the agreement, the two countries recognised the necessity to establish a framework of mutual cooperation and coordination in the fields of security and law enforcement and to provide assistance to combat all forms and types of crimes; especially hijacking, abductions, organised crime, falsification of documents, forgery of currencies, illicit economic activities, smuggling of objects of historical or cultural value, jewels, precious metals or other valuable objects, and the properties and revenues derived from organized crime and terrorism and their tracking, restriction and confiscation. Indian officials were quoted suggesting that the agreement was "just short of stationing troops (in the region)"[18]. Another official was quoted saying:

> *"Qatar has huge financial assets — gas fields, petroleum reserves — and it needs to protect them. We'll assist them in case there is a threat to its key assets"*[19]

Indian Navy warships and vessels regularly dock at Doha (Hamad Port) to further strengthen naval ties between the two countries. Indian Naval vessels have also previously participated in the Doha International Maritime Defence Exhibition and Conference (DIMDEX 2016), wherein the INS Beas guided-missile frigate took part. The Navies of either country also regularly hold professional conferences to discuss the strategic and security architecture of West Asia and the Arabian Sea. In November 2019, the Indian Navy and Qatari Emiri Naval Forces held the maiden annual bilateral maritime exercise, named 'Za'ir Al-Bahr', at Doha's Hamad Port. The exercise included the participation of INS Trikand frigate and Boeing P-8I maritime reconnaissance aircraft[20]. The exercise itself is aimed at strengthening defence cooperation in the field of fighting terrorism, piracy and security & safety of the high seas.

Oman

The Ministry of External Affairs identifies the Sultanate of Oman as a strategic partner of India in the Gulf and an important interlocutor at the Gulf Cooperation Council (AGCC), Arab League and Indian Ocean Rim Association (IORA) fora.[21] Like in other Gulf states, the Indian community in Oman has played a crucial role in building modern Oman and is highly appreciated for its detrimental efforts. Oman is also among the major oil suppliers of India, at an estimated USD 1.7 billion in the fiscal year 2018-19.

Oman is not a heavy-weight contender in the politics of the region like the neighbouring UAE, Saudi Arabia or Qatar; essentially reserving its independence from regional foreign policy alignment while also being a part of regional organisations. Muscat has projected itself as being an independent mediator in the disputes of the region and was instrumental in facilitating negotiations between the US and Iran during the Obama administration which eventually led to the signing of the Joint Comprehensive Plan of Action (JCPOA)[22]. The Omanis have also historically played the role of mediator in the everlasting Arab-Iranian disputes, both blocs with whom India engages in serious diplomatic affairs. Considering this soft power that Oman holds in the region, New Delhi hedges itself strategically in the region, partnering with Muscat.

In 2008, following then Prime Minister Dr Manmohan Singh's visit to Muscat, the governments of India and Oman reached an agreement to upgrade their bilateral ties to a strategic partnership, which was seen as a mutually beneficial and welcome step. Oman was the first Gulf state to formalise a defence and security mechanism with India, through the signing of the Memorandum of Understanding on Military Cooperation in 2005. Since then, the two Arabian Sea states have cooperated extensively in ensuring the safety and security of the shared Seas and Ocean. The Indian Navy and Royal Navy of Oman regularly conduct anti-piracy exercises and operations. In 2018, following the visit of incumbent Prime Minister Narendra Modi to Oman, an agreement was reached as per which India secured access to and services of the Port of Duqm in Oman for military use and logistical support to the vessels and warships of the Indian Navy deployed in the Indian Ocean Region[23]. The Indian Air Force and the air wing of the Indian Navy are also permitted to land at and utilise the services of Omani airports.

Oman's position as a key strategic partner in the region is highlighted by the fact that it happens to be the sole gulf state which conducts military exercises for all three services – Army, Navy and Air Force – with India. The three services of each country conduct joint training and exercises biennially. The 'Al-Najah' exercise involving the Indian Army and the Royal Omani Army, the last edition of which was held in 2017 in Himachal Pradesh. The exercise included the implementation of procedures for joint military operations to increase efficiency, develop leadership and field skills and exchange of military expertise. The Indian Air Force and the Royal Air Force of Oman last conducted aerial exercises – Exercise Eastern Bridge V – in October 2019, at AFB Masirah in Oman, with the objective of enhancing inter-operability during mutual operations between the two Air Forces and will also promote professional interaction, exchange of experience and operational knowledge[24].

In January 2020, vessels of the Royal Navy of Oman arrived at Goa to kick off the twelfth edition of the naval exercise 'Naseem-Al-Bahr' alongside the Indian Navy. During the harbour phase of the exercise, the personnel of either Navies conduct subject matter expert exchanges on professional topics, sports activities and reciprocal ceremonies[25]. The maritime exercises include facilitating inter-operability between the navies and to conduct various anti-piracy and anti-terror exercises, enhancing the security of sea lines of communication. Therefore, the Omanis play a crucial role in defining India's security architecture while also aiding India's responsibility to ensure the safe conduct of trade in the Indian Ocean Region.

Indonesia

The Republic of Indonesia is perhaps one of the most strategically located countries in the continent of Asia. It lies at the juncture where the Indian Ocean meets the Pacific. Indonesia has a strategic level of importance in the Indo-Pacific region, with its strategically important straits of 'Malacca, Ombai-Wetar, Sunda and Lombok connect the Indian Ocean Region to the Asia-Pacific. It is rightfully called the 'gatekeeper of the two oceans'. Indonesia and India share a deep-rooted connection, in history, culture and a strong and shared sense of non-alignment in the post-independence era.

India has also on several occasions come to the aid of Indonesians when most in need. In late September 2018, a series of earthquakes and subsequent tsunamis led to severe catastrophe on the island of Sulawesi. After receiving Indonesia's acceptance of foreign aid, India launched Operation Samudra Maitri, involving Indian Air Force transport aircraft and Indian Navy vessels, carrying medical personnel, relief material and supplies were dispatched to the East Indonesian island[26]. This has bought a lot of goodwill for India, among the Indonesian populace, adding on to the existing love that Indonesians hold for Indian showcase of art and culture through Bollywood.

In accordance to Prime Minister Narendra Modi's policy direction to not just 'Look East', but also 'Act East', India and Indonesia in 2018 agreed to upgrade existing ties to a new level of establishing a comprehensive strategic partnership, highlighting potential areas of cooperation in marine, economy, and socio-culture as well as discussed regional and global issues. During his state visit to Indonesia, the Prime Minister of India also said that India's Act East Policy and the vision of SAGAR (Security and Growth for all in the Region) matches Indonesian President Widodo's maritime fulcrum policy.[27]

While India and Indonesia jointly signed a defence agreement back in 2001, a new defence cooperation agreement was reached as part of the state visit of 2018. Activities relating to cooperation in the area of Defence and Security are regularly monitored and new areas discussed during the Biennial Defence Ministers Dialogue, last held in July 2020, wherein further potential areas of cooperation in the field of defence industries and defence technology were identified.[28] India and Indonesia also regularly conduct service-level staff talks alongside annual joint defence cooperation meetings. There are regular engagements at the operational level between the three services, and discussions on matters of mutual interest relating to regional security and information sharing. Engagements in capacity building through training and cooperation in the area of the defence industry are also pursued based on mutual interest.[29]

The Indian Army and Indonesian Army regularly conduct joint exercises called 'Garud Shakti' for special forces. The latest edition was conducted in early 2019 at Agra, Uttar Pradesh, with the exercise aimed at countering terrorism in urban and semi-urban backdrops, close-quarter combat and developing trust and common operational procedures at the strategic level.

The Navies of the two Republics also conduct maritime exercises regularly, called 'Samudra Shakti'. The last edition of the exercises was conducted in November 2019 in the Bay of Bengal. The joint exercises include manoeuvres, Surface Warfare exercises, Air Defence exercises, Weapon firing drills, Helicopter Operations and Boarding Operations. The harbour phase of the exercise included professional interactions in the form of subject matter expert exchanges, cross deck visits, simulator drills, planning conferences, sports and socio-cultural activities.[30] The two navies also regularly conduct patrols in the Indian Ocean Region, with the objective of ensuring the safety, security, stability and freedom of commercial shipping and international trade in the key region.

The Government of India is also planning on expanding the scope of defence cooperation with Indonesia through launching aerial exercises involving the Indian Air Force and the Indonesian Air Force, with a keen eye on China's rising regional and extra-regional sphere of operations and influence. As of now, the only aerial exercise in which India takes part with Indonesia is the biennial multilateral exercise 'Pitch Black', alongside the Air Forces of Australia, Canada, France, Germany, Netherlands, New Zealand, Singapore, Thailand, Malaysia and the United States.

India also cooperates with Indonesia in the sphere of space collaboration. In 2002, the Indian Space Research Organisation (ISRO) signed a Memorandum of Understanding with the National Institute for Aeronautics and Space (LAPAN) of Indonesia for cooperation in the peaceful uses of outer space. Cooperation in this sphere reached a new height of the two countries' strategic partnership with the launch of two Indonesian satellites LAPAN A2 in September 2015 and LAPAN A3 in June 2016, from Sriharikota Range in India.

As such, the future of Indian security plans and in efforts of making concrete the Government of India's SAGAR initiative, as well as part of plans to counter Chinese expansion into the Indian Ocean Region, Indonesia could perhaps be among the most important players.

Singapore

The city-state of Singapore is perhaps one of the countries with which India shares strong relations on all levels, ranging from culture, to politics, to military ties, and takes holds a certain degree of precedence in the determination of Indian foreign policy. Singapore too places India as a crucial pillar of their foreign policy. Relations after the independence of Singapore in 1965 were particularly close as the founding Prime Minister of Singapore Lee Kuan Yew looked up to India to help achieve his objectives of nation-building, regional security and international recognition.[31] The island country is situated at the outer end of the Malacca Straits and acts as one of the most important trade hubs in Asia and the world. Like India, Singapore is also critical of the gradual rise in China's assertive and aggressive behaviour in the region. With the establishment of airfields on shoals in the South China Sea, the People's Republic of China reserves the ability to strike the island nation in less than an hour.

With this in mind along with the fact that Singaporeans barely have any territory to fall back to, the Government places the Chinese dilemma as a top priority in their policy-making processes, bringing the United States plus allies and India to the forefront of any relevant discourse. At the same time, Singaporeans are cautious of endorsing initiatives that may seem to be of anti-China nature, with whom the island nation shares economic and cultural ties.

In 2015, India and Singapore celebrated 50 years of diplomatic relations. In November of that year, on an official visit to the island nation, Prime Minister Modi and Prime Minister Loong agreed to take relations to the next level and in a joint declaration signed the India-Singapore Strategic Partnership. As part of the visit, several bilateral agreements were reached, including in the spheres of defence, maritime security, cyber-security and narcotics trafficking. Before this too, India and Singapore had been cooperating in the field of military and security affairs, given the common threats in way of terrorism, maritime piracy and the safety and stability of sea lines of communications, alongside the ever-increasing Chinese threat. The Defence Cooperation Agreement was signed in 2003; the signing of the strategic partnership in 2015 revised this and further provided for more personnel exchanges, visits and training courses, intelligence exchanges and revised importance for the defence policy dialogue, held annually as a high-level platform for discussions on bilateral defence cooperation and common security issues. New Delhi and Singapore are also committed to sharing and cooperating in the field of intelligence and in the fight against the rising threat of terror and criminal syndicates in the region.

The Indian Army and the Singaporean Army conduct exercise Bold Kurukshetra involving armoured units from either side. 2019 marked the twelfth edition of this exercise, which focused on developing interoperability and conduct of joint tactical operations in mechanised warfare, along with interactions and exchanges of professional knowledge among personnel, enhancing mutual understanding and cooperation[32]. The two Republics' air forces also conduct annual aerial exercises, called SINDEX. The exercise provides training to conduct air operations in realistic and challenging conditions, while also strengthen the friendship and enhance interoperability between the two air forces. To commemorate the 10th edition of SINDEX, the scope of the exercise was expanded to include an air-sea training component for the first time, with supporting assets from the Indian Navy. Apart from symbolic exercises, the Singaporean Air Force also trains alongside the Indian Air Force as part of the Air Force Bilateral Agreement, signed in 2007 and renewed in 2012 and 2017 for five-year periods. The joint training will "provide the RSAF with regular opportunities to train with the IAF's advanced Su-30 fighter aircraft, as well as many touchpoints to strengthen rapport and mutual understanding at all levels", said Singapore's Defence Ministry in a news release[33].

However, among the main scopes of military cooperation between India and Singapore remains in the maritime sphere. To this extent, the Indian Navy and Singapore Navy have been participating annually in the Singapore-India Maritime Bilateral Exercise (SIMBEX) since 1993. SIMBEX has progressed from traditional anti-submarine exercises to more complex maritime exercises such as advanced air defence operations, anti-air and anti-surface practice firings and tactical exercises. The two Indo-Pacific navies aim to strengthen mutual trust, enhance interoperability, and build greater synergy to address common maritime concerns through continued exercise and cooperation. The latest edition of SIMBEX was conducted late in November 2020 in the Andaman Sea, being conducted as a 'non-contact, at sea only' exercise in view of the Covid-19 pandemic[34]. To further bolster military ties and advance common goals such as the enforcement of a rules-based world order, with New Delhi and Singapore agreeing to permit Indian naval vessels and warships at its naval base in Changi. The India-Singapore Bilateral Agreement for Navy Cooperation allows Indian Navy vessels sailing through the disputed South China Sea or in the eastern waters of the Andaman Sea will be able to refuel, restock and, if needed, rearm at Singapore's latest naval base before continuing their mission.[35]

This negates the previous bureaucratic processes of seeking permissions from the ministries of defence and external affairs of both Republics. "I would respond categorically - not only would we be more comfortable, we would encourage the Indian Navy to visit Changi Naval base more often," said Singapore's Defence Minister Dr Ng Eng Hen who also stated that India would reciprocate the logistics support when Singaporean vessels operate in Indian waters in the Andaman Sea and elsewhere. In light of recent acts of Chinese aggression, not only against India but also against other East and Southeast Asian countries, these agreements between New Delhi and Singapore come with mutual benefits. The aim of Indian and Singaporean foreign policy has and will continue to remain mutually beneficial, while also benefiting the broader region through the enforcement of a free and open Indo-Pacific and a multilateral, rules-based world order.

Vietnam

The Socialist Republic of Vietnam entered full diplomatic ties with the Republic of India in 1972, with the end of the decades-long Vietnam War and the unification of the capitalist south within the communist north. Sharing the bond of a common colonial past, India was among the few non-communist states during the cold war to have condemned American intervention in Vietnam, while also providing aid, assistance and political support to Hanoi during the Cambodian war, which ended the reign of genocidal, deranged dictator Saloth Sâr, better known as Pol Pot. The former French colony lies just south of China, with its coast all along with the strategically important, and disputed, South China Sea. The country has fought the Chinese several times, along its border with China as well as on the shoals of the Paracel islands, making Vietnam one of the very few countries willing to stand up against any Chinese aggression and expansionism in today's day and age.

Vietnam has been keen on India taking on a bigger role in terms of security in the region and New Delhi's support for Vietnam in its dark and bloody past has helped shape Hanoi's perception of India as a reliable strategic partner for Vietnam to meet its regional strategic interest.[36] In June 2020, the People's Liberation Army ambushed an Indian Army patrol in eastern Ladakh, resulting in 20 Indian soldiers killed in action, while also sustaining casualties as high as 43 killed in action. In August 2020, the Chinese deployed the Xi'an H-6J strategic bomber to Woody island in the Paracel group, a Vietnamese territory disputedly held by Beijing. In light of such tensions and given common objectives and outlook, with similar threats as well as interests, India and Vietnam are natural allies and not just strategic partners. While neither side would want to be dragged into a conflict, both sides would benefit extensively through the further development of comprehensive strategic and military ties.

In 2009, the governments of India and Vietnam signed the Memorandum of Understanding on Defence Cooperation. The two countries participate in joint military exercises, joint campaigns on anti-piracy in the South China Sea, anti-insurgency training, periodic high-ranking visits including the expansion of cooperation in the defence and security spheres, helping build closer interaction between the two nations through regular defence dialogue, training, exercises, Navy and Coast Guard ship visits, along with the capacity building.

Vietnam is also one among the many vocal supporters of India's bid to procure permanent membership at the United Nations Security Council, while also showcasing support for and the significant importance of Indian presence in the Association of Southeast Asian Nations (ASEAN). India has also in the past provided a USD 500 million line of credit to Vietnam for the purchase of defence and military equipment made in India. This ranges from maritime patrol craft to short-range cruise missiles such as the Brahmos[37]. Apart from this, the Indian Air Force as of 2016 is also committed to training pilots of the Vietnam People's Army Air Force flying the Sukhoi Su-30 fighter aircraft. The Indian Navy also provides training to submarine sailors of the Vietnam People's Navy; both Navies operate soviet-origin Kilo-class diesel-electric attack submarines. Vessels of the Indian Navy deployed in the South China Sea also make port at Vietnamese naval bases and docks for replenishment and friendly visits. Former Vietnamese Ambassador to India was quoted saying that "Indian ships are welcome in our seas"[38], while China firmly opposes the presence of Indian vessels in what the world considers international waters, but Beijing considers as its own.

The two countries also conduct military exercises among the branches of their militaries. In January 2018, the first-ever edition of the Vietnam-India Bilateral Army Exercise (VINBAX) took place in Jabalpur, Madhya Pradesh. The exercises, unlike others, was a table-top exercise, involving the exchange of knowledge and experience in deployment, management, activities and the settlement of situations that peacekeepers may face as part of UN missions across the globe, while also promoting a sense of mutual trust, understanding, cooperation and friendship among the ranks of the armies.

While military ties among the continental and aerial branches of the services of the two countries develop, the priority area of defence cooperation between the two lies in the maritime sphere. As mentioned above, India and Vietnam share common threats coming from Beijing. The Chinese regimes illegitimate and illegal claims over the entirety of the South China Sea – through the drawn up nine-dash line – is a standing threat not only to direct disputant Vietnam but also to India, through threats to open and free commercial shipping in international waters. April 2019 saw the conclusion of the second edition of the Indian Navy-Vietnam Peoples' Navy Bilateral Exercise (IN-VPN BILAT EX) off the coast of Cam Ranh Bay, Vietnam.

The exercise involved of composite training programmes in the fields of submarine, aviation and dockyard training, aiming to strengthen confidence and inter-operability as well as sharing best practices between the two navies39. It is also important to note that India invites the Vietnam People's Navy to participate in its multilateral naval exercise MILAN, held biennially in the Bay of Bengal, participated by the naval forces of 30 countries, to enhance professional interactions between friendly foreign navies, promote a sense of 'synergy across the seas'. The latest edition of the exercise – MILAN 2020 – was postponed due to the unforeseen emergence of the Coronavirus pandemic.

Hanoi has also granted exclusive access to Indian naval vessels and warships to use Nha Trang port, which is barely 15-20 km north of Cam Ranh Bay, a strategic naval base. "The fact that not even the US, a close ally of Vietnam in the region, has been conferred this privilege underscores Vietnam's perceptions about the imperative of defence cooperation with India," says Harsh V Pant[40]. India and Vietnam both find each other at a point of political and geostrategic convergence, where China's gradual rise and expansion into the Indian Ocean Region threatens India and freedom of the seas, its continued assertive behaviour in the South China Sea – a direct threat to Vietnamese sovereignty – along with Chinese aggression along Indian borderlands is the main driver of what has the potential of being a fruitful, yet natural, strategic partnership, if not alliance.

An Assessment

India's ability to maneuverer between different conflicting agendas and goals, and yet maintain and improve its ties with countries across the board is commendable. Yet, there is much more that the country can do in ensuring that it consolidates its influence over its extended strategic environment. The creation of stable diplomatic ties and security partnerships has granted India with strong strategic partners across the globe, who see mutual benefit in aiding India's security needs. However, while this has internationalised both India's reach and partners, there is also a need for India itself to play a bigger role in its own strategic backyard, possibly becoming a net security provider for the region. In doing this, India must create the conditions within which this may be achieved. And while Efforts in this regard are already under way, with India stepping up its support for a number of multilateral fora, and bolstering bilateral ties in the region, there is still much to be done though.

India must essentially look at its strategic partnerships through both larger and singular lenses, seeking to diversify yet leverage certain partnerships in specific domains. Firstly, there is a need to assess the utility of procurement, information sharing and joint defence protocols; ensuring that the countries which are friendly with India, yet are not linked to India's strategic establishment must be. There is therefore a need for India to work on similar agreements with smaller countries that could become strategic partners in the future if properly motivated, or could pose problems in the future if not properly leveraged. This includes increased collaboration with countries such as Sri Lanka, Maldives, Seychelles, and others.

India must essentially secure its neighbourhood, granting itself the superior strategic leverage in most matters. Many countries including Sri Lanka and the Maldives have secured ties with countries like China, and could pose as strategic problems in the future. The 'string of pearls' concept has found substance in the number of agreements and reciprocal arrangement that China has initiated and secured with countries across the Indian Ocean. These facilities could essentially serve to encircle India and curb its abilities for power projection, trade and regional superiority. It is noted that India has already acknowledged these issues and is building towards them, taking on a number of countermeasures in the Indian Ocean. Firstly, through India's expanded Look East Policy, India has increased its military and strategic engagements and agreements with Vietnam, South Korea, Japan, Philippines, Indonesia, Thailand and Singapore. Additionally, India has also sought to build further on a number of strategic agreements, agreeing to develop Myanmar's Sittwe port, train its navy, build a deep-sea port at Sabang in Indonesia, create a naval base in Seychelles and also establish an agreement with Oman for a naval berthing facility at Duqm port in Oman. Moreover, India has already established a listening post and a radar facility in Northern Madagascar, and coast surveillance radar systems in Mauritius and Seychelles. Through this, India is essentially building towards its aspirations to become a net security provider in the region.

However, there is more that India can do in this regard. While the above engagements will serve to improve its strategic footprint in the Indian Ocean, India still lacks coherence in its approach to the Indian Ocean. Most of what has been outlined by the MEA and other wings of the government point to bilateral agendas, and there is a significant lack of a coherent strategy aimed at even establishing India as the net security provider for the region. This fact needs to be accounted for at the earliest and India needs to firmly establish its role in official stances as well.

India's reluctance to enter directly into military alliances with other nations is well noted, and perhaps also the best strategic stance for a country to adopt. However, India can still take the lead in highlighting the need for cooperation against non-traditional challenges on a larger regional scale, while simultaneously ensuring defence and military collaboration with smaller nations. On the one hand, India must seek to develop intelligence sharing mechanisms with the other nations in its neighbourhood and also introduce renewed initiatives aimed at multilateral collaboration against piracy, smuggling, human trafficking, illegal fishing, etc. In conclusion, India has a much further to go in securing its strategic environment, however the creation of multilateral mechanisms within which it can take the lead will prove to be highly beneficial in ensuring significant strategic autonomy and influence.

Notes

1. Chaudhury, D. (2019). India and USA conclude several landmark agreements in 2+2 ministerial dialogue. The Economic Times. Retrieved from: https://economictimes.indiatimes.com/news/politics-and-nation/india-and-usa-conclude-several-landmark-agreements-in-22-ministerial-dialogue/articleshow/72892719.cms?from=mdr
2. White, J. (2021). After the Foundational Agreements: An agenda for US-India defence and security cooperation. Retrieved from: https://www.brookings.edu/wp-content/uploads/2021/01/FP_20210111_us_india_white.pdf
3. Ministry of External Affairs. (March 2018) "Joint Strategic Vision of India-France Cooperation in the Indian Ocean Region." Media Centre, Government of India. Available: https://www.mea.gov.in/bilateral-documents.htm?dtl/29598/Joint+Strategic+Vision+of+IndiaFrance+Cooperation+in+the+Indian+Ocean+Region+New+Delhi+10+March+2018
4. Pollock, J. (October 2020). "India and France: From Strategic Partners to a Strategic Alliance." South Asian Voices. Available: https://southasianvoices.org/india-and-france-from-strategic-partners-to-a-strategic-alliance/

5. Sawhney, A. (May 2020) "India and France: A Joint Step Forward." Observer Research Foundation. Available: https://www.orfonline.org/expert-speak/india-france-joint-step-forward-66844
6. Thakker, A and Elliot S. (November 2019) "India and Japan eye the Dragon in the Room." Foreign Policy. Available: https://foreignpolicy.com/2019/11/20/china-war-navy-india-japan-eye-dragon-in-the-room/
7. Rohit, TK. (September 2019). "Work on undersea cable to connect Andamans begins. The Hindu. Avaible: https://www.thehindu.com/news/national/tamil-nadu/work-on-undersea-cable-to-connect-andamans-to-begin-in-december/article29386971.ece
8. Department of Defence. (2016). Defence White Paper. Australian Government. Accessed at: https://www.defence.gov.au/whitepaper/docs/2016-defence-white-paper.pdf
9. Department of Defence. 2020. Defence Strategic Update and Force Structure Plan. Australian Government. Accessed at: https://www.defence.gov.au/StrategicUpdate-2020/docs/2020_Defence_Strategic_Update.pdf
10. Jaishankar, D. (September 2020). "The Australia-India Strategic Partnership: Accelerating Security cooperation in the Indo-Pacific." Lowly Institute. Available: https://www.lowyinstitute.org/publications/australia-india-strategic-partnership-security-cooperation-indo-pacific
11. Ibid.
12. Ibid.
13. Pant, H. (September 2019). "Israel's arms sales to India: Bedrock of a strategic partnership." Observer Research Foundation. Available: https://www.orfonline.org/research/israels-arms-sales-to-india-bedrock-of-a-strategic-partnership-55101/
14. "Israel Fence Systems, Quick Response Team at Pakistan Borders: BSF DG" (2018) *The Economic Times*. https://economictimes.indiatimes.com/news/defence/israel-fence-systems-quick-response-team-at-pakistan-borders-bsf-dg/articleshow/60044263.cms?from=mdr.
15. Ministry of Home Affairs (Government of India) (2018) "India, Israel Joint Steering Committee Meeting on Homeland and Public Security Held". Press Information Bureau.
16. Ministry of External Affairs (Government of India). (2014). "Agreement Between the Government of The Republic of India And the Government of The State of Israel On Cooperation in Homeland and Public Issues". New Delhi.
17. PTI. (2020). "India and Israel sign agreement to expand cooperation in cyber security". The Hindu. Available: https://www.thehindu.com/news/national/india-and-israel-sign-agreement-to-expand-cooperation-in-cyber-security/article32102730.ece.
18. Srivastava, T. (2008, November 19). *Qatar defence deal good: Experts*. Retrieved from Hindustan Times: https://www.hindustantimes.com/india/qatar-defence-deal-good-experts/story-0vOb3VdyQg5JH2bQYxT06L.html
19. Ibid
20. Ministry of External Affairs, Government of India. (2020, January). *India-Qatar Bilateral Relations*. Retrieved from Ministry of External Affairs, Government of India: https://mea.gov.in/Portal/ForeignRelation/India-Qatar_January_2020.pdf
21. Ministry of External Affairs, Government of India. (2017, November). *India-Oman Relations*. Retrieved from Ministry of External Affairs, Government of India: https://www.mea.gov.in/Portal/ForeignRelation/26_Oman_November_2017.pdf

22. Quamar, M. M. (2018, June 19). *Locating Oman in India's Strategic Engagements with the Gulf*. Retrieved from Middle East Institute: https://www.mei.edu/publications/locating-oman-indias-strategic-engagements-gulf#_ftn14
23. Roy, S. (2018, February 13). *India gets access to strategic Oman port Duqm for military use, Chabahar-Gwadar in sight*. Retrieved from The Indian Express: https://indianexpress.com/article/india/india-gets-access-to-strategic-oman-port-for-military-use-chabahar-gwadar-in-sight-5061573/
24. News Services Division, All India Radio. (2019, October 17). *IAF begins Joint Exercise with Oman today*. Retrieved from News Services Division, All India Radio: http://newsonair.com/Main-News-Details.aspx?id=373088
25. Press Trust of India. (2020, January 6). *Royal Navy of Oman ships arrive in Goa for naval exercise 'Naseem-Al-Bahr'*. Retrieved from Business Standard: https://www.business-standard.com/article/pti-stories/royal-navy-of-oman-ships-arrive-in-goa-for-naval-exercise-naseem-al-bahr-120010601169_1.html
26. Ministry of External Affairs, Government of India. (2019, November). *India-Indonesia Bilateral Brief*. Retrieved from Ministry of External Affairs, Government of India: https://mea.gov.in/Portal/ForeignRelation/Ind_Indonesia_N_2019.pdf
27. Press Trust of India. (2018, May 30). *India, Indonesia to upgrade ties to comprehensive strategic partnership*. Retrieved from The Times of India: https://timesofindia.indiatimes.com/india/india-indonesia-to-upgrade-ties-to-comprehensive-strategic-partnership/articleshow/64381207.cms
28. Doordarshan News. (2020, July 27). *India, Indonesia Defence Ministers' Dialogue held in New Delhi*. Retrieved from Doordarshan News: http://ddnews.gov.in/international/india-indonesia-defence-ministers%E2%80%99-dialogue-held-new-delhi#:~:text=India%2C%20Indonesia%20Defence%20Ministers'%20Dialogue%20held%20in%20New%20Delhi,-27%2D07%2D2020&text=Both%20the%20Ministers%20agreed%20to,identi
29. Ministry of External Affairs, Government of India. (2019). *India-Indonesia Bilateral Brief*. Retrieved from Ministry of External Affairs, Government of India: https://mea.gov.in/Portal/ForeignRelation/INDIA_INDONESIA__2019.pdf
30. Indian Navy. (2019, November 11). *Indonesian Navy Bilateral Maritime Exercise Samudra Shakti Progresses in the Bay of Bengal*. Retrieved from Indian Navy: https://www.indiannavy.nic.in/content/indian-navy-%E2%80%93-indonesian-navy-bilateral-maritime-exercise-samudra-shakti-progresses-bay
31. High Commission of India, Singapore. (2016, July). *India-Singapore Relations*. Retrieved from Ministry of External Affairs, Government of India: https://www.mea.gov.in/Portal/ForeignRelation/Singapore_july_2016_new.pdf
32. Vaishnava, L. (2019, April 11). *Closing Ceremony: Indo-Singapore Joint Training Exercise Bold Kurukshetra*. Retrieved from Press Information Bureau: https://pib.gov.in/Pressreleaseshare.aspx?PRID=1570421#:~:text=The%2012th%20edition%20of%20joint,held%20at%20Babina%20Military%20Station.
33. Lim, A. (2017, January 19). *RSAF to train with Indian Air Force for another 5 years, under renewed bilateral pact*. Retrieved from The Straits Times: https://www.straitstimes.com/singapore/rsaf-to-train-with-indian-air-force-for-another-five-years-under-renewed-bilateral-pact
34. News Services Division, All India Radio. (2020, November 23). *India - Singapore Bilateral Maritime Exercise SIMBEX-20 to begin today in Andaman Sea*. Retrieved from

News Services Division, All India Radio: http://newsonair.com/Main-News-Details.aspx?id=404769

35. Som, V. (2017, November 29). *India's Warships Can Now Refuel and Rearm at Singapore Naval Base*. Retrieved from NDTV: https://www.ndtv.com/india-news/wary-of-china-india-gets-rights-to-use-singapores-latest-navy-base-1781527
36. Ao, T. (2020, March 5). *India-Vietnam Strategic Cooperation: A Key Element in India's 'Act East' Policy*. Retrieved from Diplomatist: https://diplomatist.com/2020/03/05/india-vietnam-strategic-cooperation-a-key-element-in-indias-act-east-policy/
37. Bagchi, I. (2014, October 29). *India ignores China's frown, offers defence boost to Vietnam*. Retrieved from The Times of India: https://timesofindia.indiatimes.com/india/India-ignores-Chinas-frown-offers-defence-boost-to-Vietnam/articleshow/44965272.cms
38. Agencies. (2011, September 2). *Vietnam counters Chinese aggression*. Retrieved from The Times of India: https://web.archive.org/web/20140826115301/http://www.timesnow.tv/Vietnam-counters-Chinese-aggression/articleshow/4382852.cms
39. Press Information Bureau, Government of India. (2019, April 17). Second Edition of Indian Navy-Vietnam Peoples' Navy Bilateral Exercise (IN – VPN BILAT EX) Concludes. Retrieved from Press Information Bureau, Government of India: https://pib.gov.in/Pressreleaseshare.aspx?PRID=1570838
40. Pant, H. V. (2018, April). Indian and Vietnam: A "Strategic Partnership" in the making. Retrieved from S. Rajaratnam School of International Studies: https://www.rsis.edu.sg/wp-content/uploads/2018/04/PB180409_-India-and-Vietnam.pdf

3

Internal Security Challenges

India's internal security infrastructure has been relatively stable over the past few years, with most insurgent activities showing downward trends. However, threats are perpetual and require constant monitoring and assessment, and current counter measures require constant review and upgradations. The Government of India has adopted a number of critical mechanisms in this regard, however, there is always scope for improvement. The regions that have posed numerous security threats over the past few years have been the North East of India, the Red Corridor or Left-Wing Extremism affected areas, and the state of Jammu and Kashmir. Moreover, though, the internal security of India also faces challenges from other forces and influences, such as ISIS returnees, radicalized individuals and ideological influencers

The North East

The North Eastern Region of India consists of eight states; Arunachal Pradesh, Assam, Manipur, Meghalaya, Mizoram, Nagaland, Sikkim and Tripura. The region and its security is highly critical to the state of India, as it borders four different countries (i.e. Bangladesh, Bhutan, China and Myanmar); and is connected to the rest of the country by only a narrow stretch of land, the Siliguri corridor. In Historical context, most of the region has been characterized by instability and insurgency. Largely a product of British misadministration and post-independence demands for secession and state-hood, the region was further beset by problems due to the partition of India and the flow of migrants and refugees from the newly formed East Pakistan. These problems were further complicated by the influx of refugees during the independence and formation of Bangladesh.

Gradual administrative reorganization of the region, led to demands for statehood, but also led to the formation of the states of Nagaland (1963), Meghalaya (1972), Manipur (1972), Tripura (1972), Arunachal Pradesh and

Mizoram (1978). While certain institutional arrangements, including the creation of certain states and the Autonomous Councils were made in addressing the causes for conflict in the region; they nonetheless failed to fulfil the aspirations of various ethnic groups, leading to further conflict. This has over time led to many demands for autonomy and even possible secession from India. In confronting the security forces of the state, many militant groups in the region have also sought cross-border support, procured arms and weapons, and recruited and trained a large number of youth.

The Government of India has over time sought to implement various mechanisms and measures in countering and curbing such activities undertaken by the various non-state actors. The state has deployed the Central Armed Police Forces, reimbursed the security related expenditure of the state governments, provided central assistance in the modernization of other state police forces, banned a number of "unlawful associations operating in the region under the Unlawful Activities (Prevention) Act (UAPA), declared a number of specific areas or even states as 'disturbed' for the purpose of the Armed Forces (Special Powers) Act (AFSPA) and also pursued a policy of talks/negotiations with the groups that abandon violence.[1] Additionally, the Government has also been implementing schemes aimed at the rehabilitation of insurgents who lay down their arms; providing financial assistance, incentives for weapons surrendered and vocational training.

These initiatives have largely translated into constructive results for the region, noting a significant downward trend in insurgency related violence. According to reports, the declining trend of insurgency-linked fatalities in the Northeast, which began in 2015, continued through 2019 as well. According to data compiled by the South Asia Terrorism Portal (SATP), the Northeast recorded a total of 34 fatalities (18 civilians, five Security Force (SF) personnel and 11 insurgents) in 2019, as against 73 fatalities (20 civilians, 15 SF personnel, and 38 insurgents) recorded in 2018.[2] On March 4, 2020, Union Minister of State for Home Affairs Kishan Reddy stated in the Rajya Sabha, that "the security situation in the North Eastern States has improved substantially since 2014. Compared to 2013, there has been a 70% reduction in insurgency incidents, 80% in civilian deaths and 78% in security forces casualties in the year 2019."[3] According to reports, there were 1,824 surrenders by insurgents between the year 2014 and 2019.

Another important factor to note with regards to the security of the region, has been the success of negotiations with various militant groups. The government has been in negotiations with groups like the National Socialist Council of Nagaland-Isak-Muivah (NSCN-IM), United Liberation Front of Assam-Pro Talks Faction (ULFA-PTF), and factions of National Democratic Front of Bodoland (NDFB). While it was successful in signing a peace deal with pro-talks factions of the NDBF in January 2020, it has been unable to come to an agreement with the NSCN-IM despite the signing of the Framework Agreement with the outfit in August 2015. The delay in any successful negotiation has been attributed to the members of the NSCN-IM, who have been unwilling to accept that a proposed Pan-Naga entity would be devoid of political and executive influence over the Nagaland government.

Additionally, the ULFA - Anti-Talks Faction (ULFA- ATF), which has now renamed itself as ULFA-Independent (ULFA-I) is still active in the region. It is believed that while the strength of the organization is only around 150-250 militants, they are organized into three groups and spread across camps in Myanmar, Bangladesh, the Garo hills of Meghalaya, Tirap and Changlang Districts of Arunachal Pradesh and Mon District of Nagaland. Recent attacks by the groups involve an attack on Assam Rifles personnel in Arunachal Pradesh in October, and the Assam state government has also identified a possible upcoming IT threat from the association. Additionally, ties to Yunnan Province in China have also been identified as well, placing the outfit in a critical space.

Such external influence and interference in the region are major causes for concern; especially as India notes the significant threat it faces from China. According to reports, Senior ULFA leaders have confessed that as much as 80% of their weaponry is of Chinese origin including assault rifles, pistols, cartridges, grenades, and grenade launchers. While most connections were established between the 1960s and 1990s, with pro-communist Naga militants and the Manipur People's Liberation Army, among others, the threat still remains high. In 2009, a Manipuri militant told authorities that contact remained unbroken and "sixteen platoons of militants have come back to India after getting trained in China".[4] The primary means of engagement between China and such groups is through either retired PLA soldiers or state-run factories, which then source illegal arms through Myanmar and Bangladesh into the region. As recently as June 2020, Indian officials travelled to Myanmar to express concerns over a large cache of Chinese weapons discovered in the Mae-Sot region, where weapons have been passing through and towards Rakhine and Indian insurgents for years.[5] Concerns have sparked amidst Indian officials that this marks an attempt at reigniting a relatively slower Indian insurgency movement.

This among other regional dynamics is indicative of the fact that lasting peace has seemingly remained elusive to the region, with the Northeast being classified as an area of concern. Largely due to the fact that initial mechanisms aimed at preventing and countering radicalization and insurgent activities in the region had not been implemented or instituted properly, there are also other problems that have arisen in the region over the past year. During the initiation of the Citizenship Amendment Act, the Northeast saw a number of protests, some increasingly violent in nature. According to reports, the Aung Yung faction of the NSCN-Khaplang of Nagaland extended support to the agitations.[6] While much of the protests were quelled by the COVID-19 pandemic, the repercussions of such support may still cause significant problems in the coming months.

Recommendations

Insurgent activities in the Northeast have reduced but threats to security are still high. In this regard, other than certain counter measures being carried out by the CRPF and other such forces, there is also a need to address the root problems of the issue. Political concessions may not be grantable, but socio-economic programs can be launched. Adding on to the point above, at the crux of most anti-radicalization processes must lie an emphasis on programs aimed at socio-economic problems. In this regard, there has been no coordinated approach at launching civic action programs in the North East. The Sashastra Seema Bal(SSB), and other such paramilitary forces have largely been in charge of conducting any civic action programs aimed at anti-radicalization and deradicalization.

However, recent years have shown a significant lapse in coordination, regularity and funding of programs in certain vulnerable areas.[7] In this regard, there is a need to allocate sufficient funding and resources to paramilitary forces in countering any possibilities of increased radicalization in the North East. Additionally, such programs are carried out across the North East by different paramilitary and police agencies with minimal coordination across sectors. If the threat of insurgency in the North East is to be dealt with significantly, there has to be coordination between agencies in both counter-radicalization as well as anti-radicalization.

With connection to insurgent activities in Arunachal Pradesh, a state that is currently critical to the Indian Government, there is a need to strengthen interaction and cooperation with other states and the Centre. While the state currently does not account for any active insurgent groups, there are chances of radicalization due to either spill-over effects from other states or due to neglect for marginalized populations in the state. In this regard, the GoI must encourage, facilitate and increase cooperation between the police and paramilitary forces of Assam and Arunachal Pradesh. According to statistics by the National Crime Record Bureau, the number of kidnapping and abduction cases in Arunachal Pradesh remain high. Arunachal Pradesh Police records, between January and June 2019 the State recorded 59 incidents of abduction for ransom. In the corresponding period in 2018, there were 70 such incidents in the State. There was a total of 126 incidents of abduction for ransom incidents in the State through 2018 and similar numbers were noted in 2017.[8] There is therefore no significant downward trend in such cases and the Government must reassess the situation in Arunachal Pradesh in gauging if certain counter measures or anti-radicalization mechanisms can be implemented.

With regards to insurgent groups in the region that are yet to lay down arms, the government must acknowledge and identify supporting factors that are sustaining their activity; so as to develop sufficient counter measures. In this regard, a special emphasis must be given to Chinese interference in the region, as the country approaches a critical juncture in foreign relations as well. Additionally, the government must increase protection in spheres that are not currently secure. In lieu of the Assam government identifying threats across IT sectors from groups like the ULFA-I, it is essential that government, administrative and other essential cyber infrastructures are reassessed and secured.

Finally, with regards to ensuring a stable security environment in the region, there is a need to ensure cooperation between different ethnic groups. While currently antagonistic groups may be beyond the purview of collaborative initiatives, the region has still been marked by periodic ethnic clashes according to reports; a fact that needs to be addressed on the ground. With regards to the same, there is a need for inter-ethnic dialogue and collaborative programs that are initiated by the state. If problems in vulnerable areas are to be addressed, they must first be addressed at the ground level and include periodic district wise assessments, inter-village/ethnic dialogues and collaborative projects to build community cohesion.

Left Wing Extremism

A number of Left-Wing Extremist outfits have been operating in certain pockets of the country for a few decades. In a significant development in 2004, the People's War (PW), then operating in Andhra Pradesh, and the Maoist Communist Centre of India (MCCI), then operating in Bihar and adjoining areas, merged to form the CPI (Maoist) Party. The CPI (Maoist) Party, is currently the major Left Wing Extremist outfit responsible for a majority of incidents of violence and killing of civilians and security forces and has been included in the Schedule of Terrorist Organizations along with all its formations and front organizations under the Unlawful Activities (Prevention) Act, 1967.

In addition to acts like the UAPA, the government of India has formulated the National Policy and Action Plan in 2015. The plan consists of a multi-pronged approach comprising security measures, development initiatives and ensuring rights & entitlements of local communities.[9] On the development front, several initiatives have been taken for the development of roads, installation of mobile towers, skill development, improving the network of banks and post offices, besides strengthening health and education facilities.[10] According to Union Minister of State for Home Affairs, G Kishan Reddy, in a meeting with the Chief Ministers of the affected States in 2019, steadfast implementation of the National Policy and Action Plan-2015 has resulted in a consistent decline in both left-wing extremism (LWE) and geographical spread of its influence.[11]

As part of the National Policy Action Plan, the government has initiated a number of measures in countering Left Wing Extremism; including the strengthening and upgrading of capabilities and coordination of intelligence agencies. Additionally, the Ministry of Home Affairs has initiated a number of other mechanisms as well. These include the ban on the CPI (M), strengthening of intelligence mechanisms, increasing inter-state coordination; initiation of the Security Related Expenditure Scheme; Fortified Police Stations Scheme; and the Special Infrastructure Scheme (SIS). Paramilitary forces and the CRPF also carry out a number of civic action programs in vulnerable areas.

In this regard, the Government of India has adopted an integrated and holistic approach to deal with the Left-Wing Extremist (LWE) insurgency by addressing the areas of security, development and promoting good governance simultaneously. The number of overall LWE-linked incidents also fell from 781 in 2018 to 673 in 2019. Incidents of killing also came down from 217 in 2018 to 176 in 2019. 26 of the 176 overall incidents of killing were major incidents (involving three or more fatalities) in 2019. In 2018, the number of major incidents was 28.[12] Resultant fatalities from major incidents declined from 157 (eight civilians, 36 SF personnel, and 113 Naxalites) in 2018 to 122 (nine civilians, 39 SF personnel, and 74 Naxalites) in 2019.[13] Nonetheless, the government has yet to bolster its position; especially since the rebels have shown capacities for resurgence in the past, and retain significant operational and over-ground capabilities in substantial areas where they have been active.

According to a report from April 2020, the Maoists were using the nationwide lockdown amid the coronavirus (COVID-19) outbreak to regain strength, as a large group of the rebels entered the South Bastar region of Chhattisgarh from Andhra Pradesh, Telangana, Maharashtra, Jharkhand, Odisha, West Bengal, and even Nepal. Resurgence is thus an inherent threat in LWE- affected areas.

Recommendations

Despite the number of significant programs and mechanisms launched by the centre, several deficits in the fighting forces are still apparent. According to the Bureau of Police Research & Development (BPR&D), as of 2019, there were at least 21 Police Stations in Chhattisgarh, the worst affected State, which did not have a telephone. Similarly, at least 37 Police Stations in Odisha, did not have a vehicle; and 59 Police Stations in Madhya Pradesh had no wireless/ mobile connectivity.[14] The lack of adequate resources and infrastructure for police and security personnel can also significantly affect the effectiveness and implementation of counter-radicalization measures. Additionally, in 12 LWE-affected states large police vacancies still persist, with BPR&D data from 2019 showing that out of the 1,595,680 sanctioned strength, only 1243537 policemen were in position, leaving a vacancy of 352143.[15] This paucity in personnel itself can hinder monitoring mechanisms as well as schemes laid down by the government and needs to be addressed.

Under the Special Central Assistance for most LWE Affected Districts Scheme, the Government of India approved a package of Rs. 3000 crores from 2017-2020, for the facilitation of basic infrastructure and facilities in public infrastructure and services.[16] However, since this scheme was initiated, there have been no significant updates on the sourcing of these funds towards such public infrastructure projects. There is therefore a need to assess the effectiveness and implementation of such schemes as well.

According to a 14-point policy released by the government of India in 2006, "The state governments will need to accord a higher priority in their annual plans to ensure faster socio- economic development of the naxal-affected areas. The focus areas should be to distribute land to the landless poor as part of the speedy implementation of the land reforms, ensure development of physical infrastructure like roads, communication, power etc. and provide employment opportunities to the youth in these areas." This goal has not yet been wholly recognized, as the worst LWE-affected states of Jharkhand, Chhattisgarh and Bihar are still some of the worst off in terms of the Human Development Index.

Finally, in LWE-affected areas, the rate of people seeking rehabilitation or laying down arms is lower than in other areas; possibly due to the political and ideological bearing of the groups. There is therefore a need to not only encourage surrender and rehabilitation by having in place strong incentives and an attractive rehabilitation package, but also to initiate programs at the ground level that deal with countering the ideological basis of Left-Wing Extremism. While this has been done recently according to reports by the MHA, there are no figures and reports that can substantiate the same. In 2017, the government approved a media plan for a period of 3 years i.e. from 2017-2020, aimed at countering the "false propaganda" being spread by the Maoists in LWE affected areas. As part of this program, the security forces have conducted Tribal Youth Exchange programmes, pamphlet distribution, documentaries showcasing and invested in radio jingles as well. The effectiveness of these initiatives however is seemingly only apparent on the surface and there are no reports on either implementation or effectiveness in countering or securing against the Maoist propaganda. An assessment of such programs and schemes aimed at countering the ideological aspects of LWE must therefore be done.

Jammu and Kashmir

For decades, Jammu and Kashmir has experienced extremism, insurgency, cross-border terrorism and the recent perpetuations of the influence of groups like Al Qaeda and the Islamic State. Today, while the intensity of the same is greatly reduced, the consequences of recent legislative actions could possibly lead to other threats and challenges. The Union Government of India on the 5th of August 2019 introduced a Bill in the Rajya Sabha which rescinded the special status of J&K under Article 370 and led to its reduction into two Union Territories. On the 9th of the same month, the President of India, Ram Nath Kovind gave his assent to the bill and the Jammu and Kashmir Reorganisation Act, 2019 was introduced. This act split the state into the Union Territories of Ladakh (without a legislature) and Jammu and Kashmir (with a legislature).

With the initiation and implementation of this act, the government also simultaneously enforced a complete lockdown in the state in apprehension of possible unrest and retaliation. During the same period, top leaders of mainstream political parties, including three former Chief ministers were put under arrest. Today, while most of the restrictions have been lifted and the Union Territories are moving back to normalcy, certain restrictions on the internet have continued.

In terms of security and stability, while initial reports have shown an escalating trend in terrorism and recruitment since 2014, there has now been a sharp downward trend in the numbers of terror related incidents. The decline terrorism has been seen in the declining fatalities across the state. In contrast with the 452 fatalities (86 civilians, 95 SF personnel, and 271 terrorists) recorded in 205 incidents of killing in 2018, there were 283 fatalities (42 civilians, 78 SF personnel, 163 terrorists) in 135 incidents of killing in 2019. Additionally, while the number of major incidents fell from 54 in 2018 to 28 in 2019, the number of overall terrorism-linked incidents also reduced to 369 in 2019 as compared to 598 in 2018.[17] Much of this is resultant out of the state induced lockdowns that have not been completely lifted.

However, it is still a worrying fact that recruitment from locals has been relatively high in the region. According to a March 14, 2020, report, of the 257 militants killed in 2018, at least 142 were locals and the remaining 115, foreigners. Similarly, of the 152 militants killed in 2019, 120 were locals. In 2020, out of 24 militants killed in Kashmir, 21 were locals. Nonetheless recruitment had also reduced comparatively with only a total of 28 recruitments between August 2019 and January 2020 as compared to 105 during January 2019 and August 2019[18]. In accordance with this and in indication of an improving internal security situation the Union Government issued an order for the withdrawal of around 72 companies of the Central Armed Police Forces, including withdrawal of CRPF, CISF and SSB forces.[19]

Nonetheless, the security of Jammu & Kashmir and Ladakh are also dictated by cross border problems and external forces. While strategic incursions were made by China across the Line of Actual Control (LAC) at Galwan, on the Line of Control in the Jammu region, there have been numerous ceasefire violations. These violations have in fact shown an upward trend with 3186 incidents reported as of September. According to official reports and data, there were a total of 3168 ceasefire violations in 2019 as compared to 2140 in 2018, 881 in 2017 and an even lower number of 449 in 2016.[20] Additionally, 242 incidents of cross-border firing were also reported along the Indo-Pakistan Border from January to August 2020. Nonetheless, the security situation in the region has improved and is within control of the Indian security forces.

The security situation however cannot be merely seen in the form of securitization and militarization of regions. A comprehensive and complete security situation in the region cannot only be assessed or countered by only addressing problems of terrorist incursions, local terrorist recruitment, ceasefire violations and infiltration. There is also a need to understand and address problems of radicalisation, alienation, political disenchantment, social disruptions, community cohesion and national integration. In this regard, the encouraging trends in security consolidation in the region have in fact coincided with a curtailment of a number of freedoms and political rights, the lack of which can in fact induce a sense of resentment across communities and contribute towards radicalization in the new Union Territories.

The Government of India has addressed a few of the issues highlighted above by introducing a number of initiatives like the Special Industry Initiative UDAAN, the Prime Minister Development Package for J&K, Relief and Rehabilitation to Kashmiri and Jammu Migrants, both in the region and in Delhi/NCR, relief to displaced families from Pakistan Occupied Jammu & Kashmir and relief and compensation for border populations affected by cross border firing and ceasefire violations.[21] Much like the UDAAN initiative which is aimed at enhancing the skills and employability of unemployed youths in the region, the government has also sanctioned financial assistance aimed at women empowerment in the J&K by introducing training in handicraft, agriculture, energy and other activities.[22]

With regard to China, incursions across the border were made in June this year, leading to a serious escalation of border and diplomatic tensions between the two countries. This has in fact resulted in a re-militarization of the region, with an increased number of forces being deployed in the region. There is thus a direct correlation between border tensions and the internal security framework of the region; a fact that serves to also show how India's national security strategy must be highly comprehensive in its scope.

Recommendations

It has thus become increasingly evident that security threats from Jammu and Kashmir could emanate out of both internal and external trends, and a review of either dynamics must therefore be done. At the lowest level, there is a need for the restructuring of local governance institutions; allowing for more funds to Panchayats at the village level and blocks at the district levels. This would ensure that there is reduced chances of radicalization and revolt from lower-level communities that may pose a significant threat as being susceptible to terrorism and radicalization. The first step in tackling political contestation and retaliation from local populations is to ensure that socio-economic processes are smoothened.

Additionally, while the government would be unable to hold local elections in the near future, there is nonetheless a need for demonstrative policies that would be aimed at socio-economic issues. The imposition of a new demonstrative structure that includes provisions for avenues of education and employment would serve to increase the affinity of local populations towards the government of India. The reinvigoration of employment exchanges, better information services and easy verification would help increase employment in Kashmir and reduce chances of retaliation. These recommendations may require the ensuring of additional funding from the government of India, but it would nonetheless facilitate a vision of long-term stability and security in the region.

In this regard, while the government focuses on increasing both political and social stability in the region, it must emphasize smooth function of the alternate governance mechanisms that have been initiated post the abrogation of Article 370. The alternate governance mechanisms will face significant stress under public unrest and there is therefore a need for outcome-based budgeting and allocation of funds for infrastructural development. In this regard, under the economic mandate there must also be renewed efforts towards the integration of the union territories with the Indian market in a more cohesive way.

On the core security issues of terrorism as well, along with the current approaches adopted by the security forces, there is also a need for an inclusive approach towards deradicalization and reduction of terrorism in the state. The suppression of terrorists today has decreased their activities, yet the core concerns have not been addressed, making certain ex-militants susceptible to ideology and other influencing factors. Militants who have laid down arms need to be put into consultative processes aimed at engaging them with local communities which would help in countering their resurgent militancy. In this regard, it is essential that the local community, religious figures and psychologists are integrated into the de-radicalization mechanisms so that elements from across the social spectrum may help reintegrate ex-militants into society.

Finally, while it is only through socio-economic programs and consolidated de-radicalization and ani-radicalization mechanisms that public unrest can be quelled, there is also a need to ensure that this happens in absence of certain factors. In this regard, the utility and influence of political parties in these development processes must be kept at a minimum so as to ensure that polarization is minimized and the local populations are engaged more efficiently.

Institutional Mechanisms

In lieu of the number of internal security challenges that the country faces, the government has initiated a number of mechanisms and measures in ensuring India's internal security across regions. In overall assessment, these mechanisms have proved to be beneficial in reducing extremism across India, ensuring a positive step towards security in key areas across the country. Among other initiatives, the government launched the National Investigation Agency in 2008, the Multi Agency Centre, The National Intelligence Grid and the Combating Financing of Terrorism Cell. However, among other issues, most of these agencies are short of cadres which can stay in the institution for longer periods. Thus, in addition to other propositions, there is a need for skill and investigative cadres to be trained and inducted at early stages.

The National Investigation Agency

The NIA was introduced in the aftermath of the 2008 terrorist attacks in Mumbai, under the NIA Act of 2008; aimed at "constituting an investigation agency at the national level to investigate and prosecute offences affecting the sovereignty, security and integrity of India, security of State, friendly relations with foreign States and offences under Acts enacted to implement international treaties, agreements, conventions or resolutions".[23] The NIA is empowered to deal with terror related activities across the country, without the special permission of States. As per the 2019 amendment, the agency is permitted to investigate offences related to (i) counterfeit currency or bank notes, (ii) manufacture or sale of prohibited arms, (iii) cyber terrorism, (iv) human trafficking and (v) offences under the Explosive Substance Act of 1908, in addition to arrests made under the UAPA or other criminal acts. As of 2019, the NIA has listed a number of organizations as terrorist organizations under the UAPA. A total of 45 NIA Special Courts have been constituted in the States and Union Territories of India. Additionally, the government has established a vertical LWE cell in the NIA to tackle LWE related offences.

The Unlawful Activities (Prevention) Act

The UAPA was introduced in 1967 to "provide for the more effective prevention of certain unlawful activities of individuals and associations dealing with terrorist activities." While the act was initially directed at countering and identifying only the association of individuals to certain Terrorist organizations, an amendment in 2019 has broadened the scope of the act to encompass the acts of individuals identified by the government and its agencies as terrorists as well. With regards to legal measures by the state, the Terrorist and Disruptive Activities (Prevention) Act of 1985 and the Prevention of Terrorism Act of 2002 were other acts that were introduced regarding the same.

As stated elsewhere, according to reports, out of the near 67,000 people arrested under the TADA, only 8000 were put on trial, out of which only 725 were convicted.[24] In 1990, around 5000 people were charged under the TADA in Gujarat, even though the state witnessed fewer terrorist acts as compared to Kashmir and Punjab.[25] There have been reports citing the discriminatory use of the act against certain religious groups. Similar allegations were raised against the Prevention of Terrorism Act of 2002 which saw random individuals being charged under the Act on the pretext of terrorism. Within 8 months of its initiation, the act saw over 940 arrests being made, with "special discrimination" against Muslims. In this regard, the UAPA has shown signs of following similar trends. Not only have the number of people charged under the act increased, but there have also been reports of wrongful detainment. The cases of Mohammed Aamir Khan,[26] Arun Ferrirera[27] and many others are indicative of the same.

Recommendations - The implementation and usage of such legal frameworks need to be re-assessed and made more definitive. Firstly, charges made under the UAPA must be made taking into cognizance the fact that processes of deradicalization, counter-radicalization and anti-radicalization are highly distinct. Therefore, uniform legal penalties cannot be applicable in all scenarios. The implementation of penalties or counter measures must be akin to the scale of radicalization, so that there is no risk of further radicalizing individuals or increasing feelings of injustice. The wrongful detainment or implementation that these acts have been prone to, can become counterproductive by contributing towards fanaticism and radicalization. Finally, in lieu of the number of cases pending, there is a need to set up fast track courts to address issues of wrongful detainment and repatriations for those individuals that have been charged under the UAPA, TADA or POTA.

Anti-Terror Units

Anti-terror squads have shown significant progress in achieving goals set forth in tackling and implementing deradicalization and counter radicalization measures in a few states across India. Earlier in 2016, the Union home Ministry had asked a number of states to draw up a comprehensive strategy in countering attempts by international terrorist organizations. Only Kerala and Maharashtra have established and set up comprehensive policies and mechanisms since then.

The Maharashtra ATS has undertaken a number of initiatives aimed at counter-radicalization and de-radicalization; aimed at both individuals and communities. As per a 2019 report, the ATS had succeeded in reintegrating almost 114 men and six women who had been influenced by extremist ideologies, and established a number of training centres for radicalized individuals.[28] In these programs, the ATS has integrated elements from both the state and society; including the respective families, counsellors, psychologists and clerics. Additionally, as of 2018, it had also banned around 500 websites that were found to be promoting radical ideologies. The state government has also initiated a number of community level programs, aimed at integrating National Cadet Corps training, Bharat Scouts and Guides, cross-cultural language integration and mainstream media outlets that were meant to propagate mainstream views.[29]

Similarly, in Kerala, the integration of religious as well as community level actors within the deradicalization processes have proved to be beneficial. Senior police officials claim that nearly 3000 individuals have been deradicalized and are being monitored across 21 government centres.[30] Kerala has made a number of terror related arrests, and the influence of the Islamic State has also been high on online platforms. The Kerala ATS has thus also been initiated as a body which would focus on scouring the internet for suspect activity, tracking the movement of chemical and electrical components and increasing coastal surveillance.[31] Other states like Gujarat and Karnataka have also initiated such squads, however, there has been no significant updates or progress on the same.

Recommendations - In bolstering the internal security of the country, there is a need to integrate such anti-terror squads into the security frameworks of other states as well. The premise of these ATS' to adopt both hard as well as soft approaches towards radicalization can be replicated as a constructive measure in other states as well. It is to be noted that the sole use of hard counter measures may not always ensure deterrence and can often serve to be counterproductive and increase radicalization. In line with this, there is also no national approach aimed at the coordination of such Anti-terror squads or even the institution of the same in vulnerable and affected states. Furthermore, a national strategy must adopt similar measures in tackling radicalization and extremism, so as to address each case specifically based on the degree of radicalization. Additionally, while the cyber space needs to be increasingly monitored in ensuring that extremist content and sites do not perpetuate radicalization, there is also a need to launch counter-initiatives that can be aimed at the same. The need for neutral counter narratives will prove to be essential in protecting against extremist ideologies being increasingly spread online.

Notes

1. Ministry of Home Affairs (2019). "Annual Report 2018-2019." Government of India. Available: https://www.mha.gov.in/sites/default/files/AnnualReport_English_01102019.pdf
2. "Insurgency North East – Assessment 2020." South Asian Terrorism Portal. Available: https://www.satp.org/terrorism-assessment/india-insurgencynortheast
3. Reddy, K. (March, 2020). "Security Situation in North East has improved substantially." First Post. Available: https://www.firstpost.com/india/security-situation-in-north-east-has-improved-substantially-80-drop-in-civilian-deaths-from-2013-to-2019-union-minister-g-kishan-reddy-tells-rs-8118051.html
4. Dutta, Prabhash K. 2020. *Chinese PLA link behind Manipur ambush?* July 31. https://www.indiatoday.in/news-analysis/story/chinese-pla-manipur-assam-rifles-1706325-2020-07- 31.
5. "China's Push of Weapons into Myanmar, India Threat to Regional Security, Intelligence Agencies Tell Govt." News 18. Available: https://www.news18.com/news/india/china-pushes-weapons-into-myanmar-india-threatens-regional-security-3089723.html
6. Nathanael, MP. The Nagaland deadlock: With the threat of China looming over, peace talks with NSCN-IM must not be allowed to lose momentum. The Indian Express. Available: https://indianexpress.com/article/opinion/the-nagaland-deadlock-7126575/
7. PTI. (January 2020). "SSB stops allowances to troops for 2 months due to paucity of funds." India Today. Available: https://www.indiatoday.in/india/story/ssb-borderforce-payments-troops-delay-1640180-2020-01-25
8. "Insurgency North East – Assessment 2020." South Asian Terrorism Portal. Available: https://www.satp.org/terrorism-assessment/india-insurgencynortheast
9. Ministry of Home Affairs (2019). "Annual Report 2018-2019." Government of India. Available: https://www.mha.gov.in/sites/default/files/AnnualReport_English_01102019.pdf
10. Ibid.
11. PIB Delhi. (July 2019). "Substantial decrease in LWE Related Violence: Kishan Reddy." Ministry of Home Affairs. Available: https://pib.gov.in/PressReleasePage.aspx?PRID=1580083
12. "Insurgency Assessment -2020." South Asian Terrorism Portal. Available: https://satp.org/terrorism-assessment/india-maoistinsurgency
13. Ibid.
14. "Data on Police Organizations." (January, 2019). Bureau of Police Research and Development. Available: https://bprd.nic.in/WriteReadData/userfiles/file/202001301028101694907BPRDData2019-19forweb-2.pdf

15. Ibid.
16. Ministry of Home Affairs (2019). "Annual Report 2018-2019." Government of India. Available: https://www.mha.gov.in/sites/default/files/AnnualReport_English_01102019.pdf
17. "Jammu & Kashmir: Assessment – 2020." South Asian Terrorism Portal. Available: https://www.satp.org/terrorism-assessment/india-jammukashmir
18. Ibid.
19. Ibid.
20. Tiwari. (September 2020). "Ceasefire violations: 3186 incidents reported a long Line of Control in Jammu region since January 2020, says centre." Zee News. Available: https://zeenews.india.com/india/ceasefire-violations-3186-incidents-reported-along-line-of-control-in-jammu-region-since-january-2020-says-centre-2309692.html
21. Ministry of Home Affairs (2019). "Annual Report 2018-2019." Government of India. Available: https://www.mha.gov.in/sites/default/files/AnnualReport_English_01102019.pdf
22. Ibid.
23. Ministry of Home Affairs (1941) "National Investigation Agency Act" Available: https://www.mha.gov.in/sites/default/files/ctcr_nationalinvestigationagency_06092019.pdf.
24. Bidwai, P. (2008) "Fighting Terrorism After Jaipur." Transnational Institute. Available: https://www.tni.org/my/node/13316
25. Gehlot, N. (1994) India and Human Rights: Emerging Realities, 55 (4).
26. Mander, Harsh. (2016) "Framed as A Terrorist: Mohammad Aamir Khan's 14 Years Behind The Bars". Hindustan Times. Available: https://www.hindustantimes.com/analysis/framed-as-a-terrorist-mohammad-aamir-khan-s-14-years-behind-the-bars/story-tjnysshmj0ycj8yxf15lrn.html.
27. Maitra, P., 2012. After Four Years, 'Naxalite' Arun Ferreira Walks Free. [Online] Hindustan Times. Available At: <https://www.hindustantimes.com/india/after-four-years-naxalite-arun-ferreira-walks-free/story-4revgk69kxanbkvirrmxfi.html>.
28. "Once Under Isis Influence, How Some Men in Maharashtra Made A Beginning". (2019) NDTV. Available: https://www.ndtv.com/india-news/once-under-isis-influence-men-in-maharashtra-make-a-new-beginning-1991231.
29. Rajput, Sagar, And Zeeshan Shaikh. "Maharashtra Police Deradicalisation Project: Core Curriculum Step by Step". (2019) The Indian Express. Available: https://Indianexpress.Com/Article/India/Maharashtra-Police-Deradicalisation-Project-Core-Curriculum-Step-By-Step-5873952/.
30. Routray, B. (July 2019) "Islamic State Returnees: India's Counter-radicalization vs Deradicalization Approach." ISPSW. Available: https://css.ethz.ch/content/dam/ethz/special-interest/gess/cis/center-for-securities-studies/resources/docs/ISPSW_632_Routray.pdf.
31. Anand, G. (2019) "Kerala Police To Form Anti-Terrorist Squad". The Hindu. Available: https://www.thehindu.com/news/national/kerala/kerala-police-to-form-anti-terrorist-squad/article27277223.ece.

4

Modernisation of the Defence Forces

It is hard for any of us to accept the truth. While we take pride in our strength and capabilities, it is vital for us to accept that India has for a long time, longer than comfortable, been the victim of foreign aggression; and it continues to remain so today. The golden bird of the old world, India has fought and lost battles and wars against foreign aggressors such as the Islamic invasions and caliphates into the subcontinent, the arrival of the British and other western powers and also the aggression that India continues to face from its neighbours all along the terrestrial international borders. In all this, the Indian people have also celebrated several victories against foreign aggressors: the Umayyad caliphate, the glorious victories of the Marathas and the Sikhs over the Mughals, the Durranis and so on.

In modern times, the Republic of India, which emerged from the cloudy history of imperialism and colonialism, won more victories than ever before. In all of its wars against its rogue neighbour Pakistan, the Indian Armed Forces won definite and honourable victories. The expansionist regime in Beijing, however, has – without a doubt – been the greater threat. In 1962, the Chinese managed to steamroll over Indian positions in Ladakh and across the northern Indo-Sino land border. As a result, the Chinese have been occupying the Aksai Chin region since over sixty-years. In 1967, the Indian Armed Forces gave the People's Liberation Army a bloody nose at the Nathu La and Cho La clashes, wherein, the Chinese suffered a whopping 340 KIA, ultimately leading to their withdrawal from sovereign Indian territory. The conflict was seen as a sign of tremendous improvement of the fighting capabilities of the Indian Army, just five years after it had lost to the same adversary.

India is at a very crucial juncture, faced with the threat of a two-front war. An ever-aggressive China is building up a permanent military presence along the Indo-Sino border with what can be seen as being of offensive nature. The Pakistanis, even though on the FATF grey-list, are sparing neither a second, nor a penny on funding and funnelling funds toward causing chaos, havoc and death in the Kashmir valley. What India and its government chooses to do today will determine the future path of the country. Choosing to stand down to foreign aggression will forgo national interests and undermine the sovereignty of the Indian nation and people. Choosing to stand down will also diminish India's image as a powerful state with a say in the happenings of the international arena. Choosing to stand down and remaining internally divided will lead to a repeat of history, in which foreign aggressors conquered a divided people.

India, however, has chosen to stand up; to not stand down and to not give in. Since the past few years, the Government of India has invested billions into the only tool that will have a say in safeguarding India's interests and sovereignty against foreign aggression. The Indian Armed Forces are in the coming years going to continue to undergo modernisation policies, directed towards the purchase of modern warfare equipment as well as the complete revolutionising and optimisation of the structure of the organisations. The aim is to reshape all branches of the Indian Armed Forces into a lean, mean fighting force capable of safeguarding the nation against the ever-evolving nature of threats faced by the state.

Current Endeavours and Progress

With the current and future nature of threats in mind, the tri-services are going to undergo a serious revamp to modernise not only their fleets and equipment, but also their structural organisation: from the tactical-level to the strategic-level. Any modernisation of the armed forces will require the government and the armed forces themselves to develop a plan with long-term objectives which will change the perception of threats, revolutionise current military & security doctrines, and at the same time work in accordance to the allocated economic budget, capable of supporting the military expenditure in mind.

In September 2019, the Government of India finalised plans to invest USD 130 billion in the modernisation of the armed forces[1]. This will include the procurement of a vast array of weapons systems and platforms that may include personal weapons, armoured fighting vehicles, drone/unmanned vehicular technology, aerial defence systems and sensors, aircraft and naval vessels. The Government has fast-tracked the procurement of a lot of modern equipment which has greatly enhanced the fangs of the fighting force. It has also supported the indigenous development of modern technology, while also inviting foreign direct investments and technology into the defence manufacturing complex.

Indian Army

The government is looking to modernise all branches of the armed forces. However, the primacy of the Indian Army is crucial, considering that any clash with either neighbour – China or Pakistan – will be fought largely by ground forces.

The single most important branch of the ground forces is the infantry. In that regard, tremendous efforts are being made to modernise. In October 2017, the Ministry of Defence approved the beginning of the processes of acquiring 700,000 assault rifles, 44,600 carbines and 44,000 Light Machine Guns. For rifles, the Indian Army has begun to search for options beyond the Ordinance Factory Board's listings. Foreign options such as those from Russia and the United States match the requirements of the armed forces.

In a joint venture with Russia's Kalashnikov Group, OFB founded Indo-Russia Rifles Factory at Amethi, Uttar Pradesh, which will produce 750,000 AK-203s. The weapon is a 7.62×39 mm automatic assault rifle with an effective firing range of 300 m and a firing rate of 700 RPM. The rifle will replace the ageing INSAS standard issue rifle and will become the organic mainstay of the Indian Army. Of the 750,000 rifles that the factory will produce over a period of 10 years, the Army will receive over 730,000 rifles, the Air Force will receive 29,000 and the Navy will receive 13,600[2].

The Armed Forces will also be procuring American-made rifles. A deal for procuring 72,400 Sig Sauer 716 assault rifles had been made in February 2019 at a cost of around INR 700 crore[3]. The weapon is a 7.62×51mm automatic rifle with an effective firing range of 600 m. The Indian Army received the first batch of 10,000 of these rifles in December 2019. Of the total, 66,000 will be operated by the Army, while the Air Force and the Navy will operate 4,000 and 2,000 rifles, respectively[4]. In light of heightened tensions along the Chinese frontier in the North, the Defence Acquisition Council approved the fast-track acquisition process of an additional 72,000 Sig Sauer 716 assault rifles at a cost of INR 780 crore[5]. These advanced rifles will give the Indian Army the much-needed edge in defending against the Chinese aggressors sitting on the other side of the Himalayas in Tibet.

The acquisition of both the Russian-origin AK-203 and the American-made SIG 716 show India's multilateral approach, gaining clout with both the Kremlin and the White House. The continued reliance of the Indian armed forces on Russian equipment is symbolic of India's continued strategic friendship, and not just partnership, with the Russian Federation. At the same time, New Delhi and Washington have been diversifying their relation in all fields, including cooperation in defence, technology and intelligence. The defence trade between India and the US has witnessed a significant upswing in the last few years almost touching the USD 18 billion mark in 2019[6].

Earlier this year, in March 2020, the Ministry of Defence signed the papers for the purchase of 16,479 Israeli-made IWI Negev LMGs for a deal worth INR 880 crore. The 7.62×51mm light machine gun can fire at a rate of 1,050 RPM till an effective range of 800 m and a maximum range of 1,200 m. It is believed that the combat-tested weapon platform will replace the ageing INSAS LMG, which is currently used by the Indian Army. As per a statement released by the Ministry of Defence, "The provisioning of this operationally urgent and very critically needed weapon will boost the confidence of the frontline troops and provide much needed combat power to the armed forces"[7].

The Ministry of Defence had also for a long time shown interest in improving the personal armour options available to its frontline heroes. For a very long time, soldiers would be deployed in combat roles without any body armour. The incumbent government enabled defence organisations in India, such as the Defence Research & Development Organisation, to make great strides in this regard. The Make in India campaign has also opened up the defence manufacturing sector to private entities. To support the establishment and growth of the Indian defence manufacturing complex, the DRDO has shared its armour technology with private company MKU Limited. The government has decided to procure 186,000 bullet-proof jackets for the armed forces and a majority of them will be manufactured by the private firm[8].

Figuratively speaking, the weather in the Himalayas is getting hot. We have seen the deployment of heavy, main battle tanks such as the T-72 Ajeya and the T-90 Bhishma in Ladakh, alongside Infantry Combat Vehicles such as the BMP-2 Sarath. While ICVs are easier to operate and manoeuvre in the sharp ridges and harsh topography of the region, the heavy MBTs are not. The PLA on the other side of the Line of Actual Control has also deployed tanks in the region. The PLA tanks, however, are not MBTs, but Light Tanks. The Type 15 light tank weighs 33 tonnes, which compared to the T-72 and T-90 at 41.5 tonnes and 46 tonnes, respectively, is much lighter. This gives the PLA an edge in in-battle combat manoeuvring. While it may take a while for the Indian Army to diversify its armoured and strike corps, the Ministry of Defence has already gone ahead with a repeat order for procuring Israeli-made Spike-LR anti-tank guided missiles, with a range of up to 4 km. The emergency procurement call was sanctioned by the Ministry of Defence and the Defence Acquisition Council early in July 2020, just weeks after the Galwan Valley clash which had left 20 Indian soldiers killed in action. The Ministry of Defence received new emergency powers, which give the armed forces a free hand to procure equipment worth up to INR 300 crore on a priority basis with deliveries stipulated to be completed in three months but extendable up to six months[9].

Indian Air Force

What has made the news in recent months, however, is not the Indian Army, but the Indian Air Force. The Indian Air Force has inducted several new platforms over the last few years, including the Boeing CH-47 Chinook heavy-lift helicopter, the Boeing AH-64 Apache attack helicopter, the HAL Tejas light combat aircraft and also the Dassault Rafale multirole combat aircraft. The Chinook has greatly improved the Indian Air Force's strategic-lift capabilities, alongside the Boeing C-17 Globemaster III and the Lockheed Martin C-130J Super Hercules. The Chinook is capable of carrying heavy equipment and troops from rear airbases to frontlines. The Apache is going to revolutionise the Indian Army and the Indian Air Force's attack helicopter corps'. With the HAL LCH on its way to induction, it is high time that the Indian Armed Forces built a larger capacity for rotor attack sorties.

The Indian Air Force has been facing a shortage of aircraft and squadron strength for many years now. The Air Force has come down to just 30 combat squadrons over the years, with the retirement of ageing and failing aircraft; internal assessments state the requirement of at least 42 squadrons to defend all theatres of the nation.

The gradual addition of further Dassault Rafale fighter jets will improve the current state of the Air Force, but at merely 36 jets, it will not be enough. With the Chinese threat straying the halls of the South Block, the Defence Acquisition Council approved, on emergency basis, defence purchases worth INR 38,900 crore[10] including the purchase of 21 premade Mig-29 Fulcrum jet fighters, the upgradation of 59 of the existing Mig-29s operated by the Indian Air Force, as well as the purchase of 12 Su-30 MKI Flanker jet fighters. The Air Force will also purchase nearly 250 units of the Indian-made DRDO Astra BVR air-to-air missile, which has an operational range of 110 km.

The Chief of Air Staff – Air Chief Marshal R K S Bhadauria – has at multiple times pointed towards the importance of going ahead with another deal to acquire 83 of the Indian-made HAL LCA Tejas. The Indian Air Force will eventually be operating 123 LCA Tejas'. The Air Force is also looking to boost the development of the indigenous fifth-generation combat aircraft – the HAL Advanced Medium Combat Aircraft (AMCA). Tenders have been released for foreign manufacturers to take part under technology transfer[11]. The Air Chief Marshal also said that the Air Force and the DRDO, were developing indigenous combat systems, which included hypersonic weapons, directed energy weapons, smart wingman concepts, alternatively manned platforms, drones, and 6G technologies. ACM Bhadauria acknowledged that 'no matter how fast we move, the Indian Air Force will not reach its authorized 42 Squadron in the coming decade but becoming a 36-38 squadron force will be achieved'[12].

Drones have been playing an important role in Intelligence, Surveillance and Reconnaissance (ISR) activities and the Indian military high-command is realising its importance in future battlefields. The Air Force is also actively developing its fleet of unmanned aerial vehicles. It currently operates the Israeli made IAI Heron medium-altitude long-endurance UAV and the IAI Searcher. However, the DRDO has also stepped in the world of drones and is actively developing modern technologies for use by the military. The Rustom and Rustom II are DRDO's long-range multi-mission drones. The Rustom II was inducted by the armed forces for ISR operations and can stay in flight for 24 hours at a stretch. The DRDO is also working on developing an unmanned combat aerial vehicle (UCAV) for the tri-services, with project name autonomous unmanned research aircraft (AURA). However, not much progress has been made in this regard. The armed forces are, as such, forced to turn to options abroad, such as Israel and the United States.

Indian Navy

The Indo-Pacific is home to a lot of the major economies of the world – from India to Indonesia, to China, to Japan. It is also a strategically very important region, with several maritime chokepoints such as the Bab-el-Mandeb, Strait of Hormuz and the Malacca Strait. The Malacca Strait alone is the transit point for almost a million vessels carrying 25% of the world's trade, annually. The region (Indo-Pacific) as a whole account for 40% of the global GDP. As such, the security aspect of the region is crucial not only to India, but to all major economies of the world.

The Indian Ocean Region (IOR) is India's backyard. It is in the country and the people's best interest in both economics & trade as well as geopolitical security & stability to safeguard the maritime sphere against entities with differing interests. These entities may be Somali pirates, Pakistani 'terror boats' or even Chinese adventurism. New Delhi must make note of the alarming rate at which the Chinese are modernising their naval fleets, expanding their capabilities to assert themselves in the South China Sea and the East China Sea, with their eyes on the Pacific. The Chinese have also on several occasions ventured into the IOR. The Pakistanis, on the other hand, have also been gradually modernising their naval fleet through the purchase of Chinese and Turkish built vessels of war. As such, while the modernisation of the Indian Army and Indian Air Force take some sort of precedence over the Indian Navy, it is vital to keep in mind the evolving factors affecting the geostrategic politics of the IOR.

The Indian Navy is currently working on plans to expand and modernise the fleet and expand its scope of operations through the induction of new warships, submarines and aircraft besides expanding its overall influence in the strategic maritime zones. Under the plan, the Navy aims to have a force level of 200 ships, 500 aircraft and 24 attack submarines; at present, the Navy has around 132 ships, 220 aircraft and 15 submarines[13]. The Indian Navy aims to evolve from its current state as a buyer's navy into a builder's navy, aiming to reach the 200-vessels mark by the year 2027.

As part of the indigenisation of the Navy and Making in India, the INS Vikrant aircraft carrier, the country's biggest and most prestigious naval project, ever, enabled India to join an elite club of nations capable of designing and constructing aircraft carriers. In October 2020, the INS Vikrant – delayed due to the COVID-19 pandemic – will enter the phase of basin trials, which will test the durability of the vessel and its fitted equipment in water. If all goes well, the vessel will be scheduled to enter sea trials as early as December 2020. The Indigenous Aircraft Carrier-1 (IAC-1) – INS Vikrant will be a STOBAR (Short take-off but arrested recovery) carrier which will be able to accommodate almost 40 aircraft, of both fixed-wing and rotatory-wing configurations. It will operate Mig-29Ks in its carrier air group, alongside helicopters such as the Westland Sea King ASW and SAR, HAL Dhruv Multirole and the Kamov Ka-31 AEW.

Mazagaon Dock Shipbuilders in Mumbai and GRSE in Kolkata are building six new multirole frigates of the Nilgiri-class for the Indian Navy. Construction work on the first vessel of the class began in 2017 and is expected to be delivered to the Navy by the year 2022. It will be equipped with Barak 8 Long-Range Surface-to-Air Missiles, which were developed jointly by India with Israel. The SAM has an operational range of 100 km at Mach 2 and operational ceiling of 16 km. It can be used to defend against a variety of airborne threats including aircraft, helicopters, UAVs, UCAVs, missiles as well as ballistic missiles. The frigate will also be capable of operating the larger Brahmos supersonic cruise missile, developed jointly by India with Russia. It has an operational range of 500 km at Mach 3, with flight ceiling rated at 15 km. It is the world's fastest cruise missile currently in service.

The Navy has had several other projects over the last few years which have moved it further toward the objective of complete fleet modernisation, including but not limited to, the Kolkata-class destroyers, further addition of Talwar-class guided missile frigates with help from Russia, Kamorta-class anti-submarine warfare corvettes, Landing Platform Docks (amphibious assault Ships), as well as the Kalvari-class of submarines based on the Franco-Spanish Scorpène-class.

Smart Forces

With the evolution of warfare from first generation in the ancient world to today's fourth and fifth generations of warfare, it is nought but an absolute necessity for the Indian Armed Forces to learn and adapt to the changing face of combat. Despite this evolving nature of warfare, however, the need for traditional military strength is not going to fade away anytime soon. At the same time, the battle winning factor of future wars may not be numerical equivalence, but technological superiority. The Chief of Army Staff – General Manoj Mukund Naravane is quoted saying:

> *"We have possibly entered the era of 'contested equality', wherein technology will make unequals equal. Perhaps that is already happening -- the battle wining factor in future combat may not be numerical equivalence but technological superiority ... Icons of the 20th-century warfare like large main battle tanks and fighter aircraft are on their way out"*[14].

Modern technologies will, therefore, play the detrimental factor in determining the outcome of battles and thereby wars. The Army is already undertaking a major study on such niche technologies, which range from drone swarms, robotics, lasers, directed energy weapons, loiter munitions, as well as artificial intelligence, cloud computing & networking, metadata analysis and algorithmic warfare[15]. A senior officer (unnamed) of the Indian Army was quoted saying:

> *"There is a technology tsunami underway that will compel militaries to reorganise and restructure to fight future wars. Warfare is undergoing a sea change due to the emergence of the new domain of disruptive technologies"*[16].

At this point of time, India faces the threat of a two-front war with China and Pakistan, setting this scenario as the main dilemma of all policy decisions to be made by the South Block in the field of modernising and enhancing the capabilities of the armed forces. The incumbent government has been highly supportive of the plans to modernise the military and its command structures. The path ahead for the Indian Armed Forces will not be individual paths for each of the services, rather a path of oneness that leads to the evolution of the Army, Air Force and the Navy into an integrated fighting force. Retired Colonel Ajai Shukla, now a renowned defence analyst, in an interview with The Diplomat, spoke about how the tri-services have had a lack of coordination in operations as well as acquisitions. He says:

> *"Each of the three services tends to structure, equip, plan and prepare for single service operations. The air force, for example, accords far greater priority to equipping itself with air defence fighters than with ground support aircraft. Its stranglehold over attack helicopters, including tank killers such as the Apache AH-64E, means the army's armoured divisions must coordinate with the air force for integrating these assets into the land battle. Similarly, the navy focuses far more on capital warships – frigates, destroyers, aircraft carriers and submarines – than it does on amphibious warfare vessels that are crucial for exercising control over India's numerous island territories"*[17].

In this regard, the Government of India alongside the tri-services has implemented several new measures. One of the most prominent was the creation of the post of Chief of Defence Staff (CDS) and the creation of the Department of Military Affairs (DMA). The CDS, who will chair the Chiefs of Staff Committee will lead efforts to integrate the armed forces into the government edifice to enable them to participate fully in decision-making. Another key responsibility would be to facilitate the restructuring of military commands for optimal utilisation of resources by bringing about jointness in operations[18].

The Ministry of Defence has also been looking into bringing to life the concept of Integrated Battle Groups. The implementation of this concept will take the process of synergising the efforts of the tri-services one step ahead.

Integrated Battle Groups (IBGs) are self-sufficient, brigade-sized fighting units, which would be tasked to perform both offensive roles including cross-border operations, as well as defensive roles to repel enemy attacks. These battle groups will aim to tackle and eliminate the historical issues that the armed forces have faced in mobilisation of forces. These IBGs will ensure faster punitive and defence operations, employing a vast variety of equipment and capabilities, including artillery, armour, infantry, combat engineers, signals and other support units. Taking into consideration the diversity of India's topography and long, bitter borders, each IBG will be designed and tailored to accommodate its ascertained threat, terrain and task. The composition of every IBG would differ on the basis of the terrain where it is located — an IBG operating in a desert needs to be constituted differently from one operating in the mountains or in dense forestation[19]. At this moment, the concept of IBGs remains in the phase of tests and experimentation and not application. The 17 Corps, also called the Mountain Strike Corps, is responsible for defending the 4,000 km long border with China, from Ladakh to Arunachal Pradesh. The three IBGs anticipated under the 17 Corps are equivalent to a Brigade in manpower and capability, aimed at striking swiftly and launching controlled offensives in high altitude[20].

Major General B.K. Sharma, Director, United Service Institution of India, makes comments on the issue of establishing a second Mountain Strike Corps aimed against the Chinese threat, while also highlighting the necessity of implementing the concept of IBGs:

> *"While theaterisation is the long-term solution, but in the interim, besides additional forces for Eastern Ladakh, we need two MSC, one for Ladakh and Middle Sector and another for the Eastern command ... However, any force structuring and development should have an optimum mix of boots on ground and high-end technology. The new strike corps must be equipped with optimum ISR, long-range targeting platforms, high mobility transportation means, EW, AD and dynamic*

> *logistic support capabilities to operate in super high-altitude terrain on sustained basis, as PLA enjoys significant competitive advantage in the technologically empowered Rocket Force and Strategic Support Force"*[21].

Another important concept brought about through these comments is the implementation of theatre commands for India's armed forces. The Prime Minister's Office has tasked the Chief of Defence Staff to establish theatre commands, similar to what the United States and China currently have. As of today, the tri-services conduct operations individually and coordinate with their respective commands their objectives and situation reports. The only instance where a joint tri-service command has been set up and is currently operational is the Andaman & Nicobar Command, based at Port Blair and established in 2001 to safeguard India's interests in the strategic strait of Malacca and the larger Southeast Asia.

Theaterisation refers to placing units of the army, air force, and navy under a single Theatre Commander. The operational command of such combinations will be under one officer drawn from one of the three services. "Theaterisation of commands is imperative to integrate resources of the three services for maximising impact in any war. The geographical expanse of theatres in India demands unified commands for strategic decisions and critical outcomes that will be possible in concentrated employment of resources," said former VCOAS Lt Gen A S Lamba[22].

As per reports, the Indian Armed Forces will be divided into five theatre commands, expected to be operational by 2022:

- Northern Command
  The Northern Command will stretch from the harsh ridges of the Karakoram Pass in Ladakh, all along the 3,488 km long Line of Actual Control with China, to the easternmost outpost in Kibithu, Arunachal Pradesh.
- Western Command
  The Western Command will be handed the mandate of safeguarding the country against all threats emerging from the other side of the Indo-Pakistani border. It will stretch from the Indira Col in the Karakoram range in the north, all the way through the plains of Punjab and the Thar desert in Rajasthan, to the tips of North-western Gujarat.
- Peninsular Command
  The Peninsular command will merge the western and eastern commands of the Indian Navy, alongside the assets of the Indian Army and the Indian Air Force. The command will be mandated with the defence of Peninsular India, against threats that may emerge from the Indian Ocean and its adjoining seas.

- Maritime Command
  The Maritime Command will be tasked with safeguarding India's maritime interests and assets in the Indian Ocean Region. It will defend India's sovereignty and island territories while also ensuring the freedom and peaceful transit of trade through strategic sea lanes of communication against any external pressures, state or non-state. The Andaman & Nicobar Command is probably set to be merged with the Maritime Command.
- Air Defence Command
  The Air Defence Command will be handed the mandate of protecting Indian sovereignty over its airspace. The Air Force, Army and the Navy currently operate their individual aerial defence units and equipment. It will be the aim of this command to synergise efforts in this direction under a single commander. There is also the possibility of expanding this into an aerospace command, encompassing a larger mandate.

Recommendations

The Indian Armed Forces have been undertaking measures to modernise their capabilities as well as they can, given the tight budget allocations. This, along with the explicit objectives set forth by the central government make it an extremely tough task for defence planners and officials to allocate the tight budget appropriated to the Ministry of Defence; keeping in mind that it is not only the Army, the Air Force and the Navy, among which the budget is to be divided. The budget allocated to the Ministry of Defence also funds other affiliated organisations, including but not limited to the Coast Guard, the Defence Research & Development Organisation, the Border Roads Organisation, the Ministry itself. In all of this, policy makers must keep in mind the following broad points:

- Determine current and future national security threats and challenges.
- Establish framework outlining doctrines and national defence strategy, alongside objectives.
- Reorganise and develop existing and planned force structures as needed to execute determined objectives[23].

One of the most popular notions running around the minds of defence thinkers and analysts is that the Indian armed forces must reduce on their current manpower. Like in industries and economics, entities can be of either manpower-intensive nature, or technology-intensive nature. One can either have workers work at factories or have a mix of workers aided with modern technologies work at factories. It is all about optimisation and making the system more efficient, taking into consideration the respective availability of resources among other factors and conditions. Similarly, slashing of manpower would be an advisable decision to make if the armed forces – whether the Army, the Air Force or the Navy – had already reached or were approaching the end stages of modernisation and parity with the forces of leading militaries such as that of the United States and China.

While technology will be the main driver of militaries – including that of India's – in the future, as of today, it would not be an advisable step to consider slashing down the Indian military's reliance on manpower. Most of the military challenges that India faces today come from the northern parts of the country which are covered in mountainous topography. India may have satellite coverage and other measures to conduct reconnaissance in these challenging landscapes, but once intelligence is gathered, there are only so many options available to tackle any detected threats. Unfortunately, in the short-term and mid-term assessment of options, the intensive manpower available to the armed forces is the only option available to employ in such scenarios. If slashing of manpower to make a leaner and meaner fighting force is the end goal, then it becomes a necessity to foster and develop other options to employ. The development of a strong Army Aviation Corps and a stronger air-ground attack wing (including rotatory) of the Air Force should be one of the major priorities for the armed forces.

In this regard, the Army and the Air Force have begun inducting Boeing AH-64E Apache Guardian attack helicopters. The indigenously developed HAL Light Combat Helicopter is also in its final test phases. Prototypes of the LCH were recently deployed in Ladakh. "It is the lightest attack helicopter in the world designed and developed by HAL to meet the specific and unique requirements of Indian armed forces reflecting the crucial role of HAL in Atma Nirbhar Bharat" said HAL chairman R Madhavan[24]. The helicopter, however, still requires further modifications to better suit the role it will play in the future dynamics of the Indian battlefield. The military must also look into the development of its unmanned aerial capabilities to further gain an edge in the application of modern military technology in the harsh conditions of the Himalayas all along the northern frontier, Ladakh and Jammu & Kashmir. Until these fields are developed to an extent of being able to operate standalone sorties, it is inevitable for the Northern frontier to remain a manpower intensive one.

In the plains and deserts of the Western border, in Gujarat, Rajasthan and the Punjab, the army operates mechanised and armoured forces which deter the threat of offensives coming from Pakistan. In this field as well, the military will remain manpower intensive. While quality of strength and capabilities will remain paramount, the quantity and sheer size of the force will also play a detrimental factor in determining the outcome of any war-like eventualities. It is only after further advanced technologies are fully developed and capable of replacing conventional military units after being fully-tested and learnt, that the military can consider slashing down on manpower. The concept of Integrated Battle Groups is still under development and is not expected to be implemented before 2021-22, so that South Block can be absolutely confident in the efficiency and effectivity of the concept before implementing it.

In the field of defence acquisitions, India must look to increase capital investments in equipment and platforms to be used by its soldiers. There is a range of equipment that is already in the acquisitions process' pipeline. There is, however, the need for a lot more modern equipment and platforms across all three services. One such requirement can be in the field of additional protection for soldiers. As of today, it is only the strike corps and armoured corps of the Indian Army which operates the BMP-2 Sarath – an Infantry Combat Vehicle (ICV). A majority of the infantry units across the various regiments still rely upon "soft-skinned" trucks, such as the Tata LPTA and Ashok Leyland Stallion series of trucks; these qualify as only motorised infantry units. The benefits of the Sarath are bifold: first, it provides a more definitive degree of protection to its occupants and second, it can be used for more purposes than just troop transport and can be used in offensive roles. The amphibious Sarath comes armed with a 30 mm cannon, with the ability to launch anti-tank guided missiles as well.

In recent news, the DRDO conducted a successful test of the Nag ATGM, which will soon be inducted into the Indian Army, with the BMP-2 Sarath being a compatible platform for employment of the munition. On June 2, 2020, the Ministry of Defence signed the papers for the procurement of an additional 156 units of the BMP-2 Sarath, which is manufactured locally by the Ordnance Factory Board's Medak factory, for an INR 1,094 crore deal[25]. While the current government has done a lot, there are still several other capital assets, the acquisition of which the forces could benefit from. The current government has also enabled the private sector to enter the restricted space of defence manufacturing in India. It should continue with this objective and pave the way for the establishment of a private defence manufacturing apparatus in India. This will boost not only the economy in terms of job creation and research & development of indigenous technology, but also make the armed forces more Atma Nirbhar, and less reliant on foreign agencies for the procurement of weapons and allied platforms.

Returning now to policy, which must – now more than ever – be directed at countering the threat emerging from Beijing. A politically cemented dictator with the second strongest military in the world with his eyes on all neighbours is the single largest threat that the Republic of India and her sovereignty faces today. In this regard, it is crucial for South Block to revive plans for reviving the plans for the establishment of a second Mountain Strike Corps, directed to deter Chinese aggression along the Himalayan border with the aggressive country. Currently, the XVII corps is the only such army formation in the role. It is currently stationed at Panagarh in West Bengal. China has been constructing an extensive transport network including both roadways and railways, connecting the several existing and under construction outposts along the disputed Indo-Sino border. At the same time, Indian construction activities along the same border, in a bid to establish a balance, are met with aggressive resistance from the PLA. This is primarily the reason why India has locked horns with China since the past seven months now. The Mountain Strike Corps, which costed INR 65,000 crore to set up initially, is currently facing a cash crunch, with only a single division active under its command.

The Ministry of Defence must act on an urgent basis not only to fund the existing 17 Corps but must also act on reviving old plans on the establishment of a second. "Thinking of expenditure at the cost of losing sovereignty is not a good idea" says Ex-COAS General J J Singh[26], when asked regarding the issue. Former General-Officer-Commanding of the Srinagar-based 15 Corps Lt Gen Satish Dua says, "Force structures are decided by operational requirement which depends on threat analysis, which in turn is a function of terrain and force application. Plains and deserts can't be compared with mountains. It is not about number of forces arrayed against an adversary. Forces are adequate, we need to modernize them more. Capability building is more important than bean count"[27]. Through Lt Gen Satish Dua's understanding of the dynamics in the Himalayas, analyses can be drawn that eventually, with the development and inculcation of modern technologies and capabilities in the long-term will replace the current and short-term requirements of a manpower intensive doctrine.

Notes

1. PTI. (2019, September 10). India to spend a whopping USD 130 billion to modernise forces. Retrieved from The Economic Times: https://economictimes.indiatimes.com/news/defence/india-to-spend-a-whopping-usd-130-billion-for-military-modernisation-in-next-5-7-years/articleshow/71053542.cms?from=mdr
2. Katoch, L. C. (2020, January). New Assault Rifles After 15 Years. Retrieved from SP's Land Forces: http://www.spslandforces.com/story/?id=677&h=New-Assault-Rifles-After-15-Years#:~:text=The%20Army%20is%20to%20get,be%20signed%20in%20early%202020.
3. India Today. (2019, February 12). Govt signs mega Rs 700-crore deal to buy 72,000 modern rifles for Indian Army. Retrieved from India Today: https://www.indiatoday.in/india/story/sig-sauer-deal-indian-army-72000-rifles-rs-700-crore-1454371-2019-02-12

4. Negi, M. S. (2019, December 11). Indian Army received first batch American assault rifles for operations in Jammu and Kashmir. Retrieved from India Today: https://www.indiatoday.in/india/story/indian-army-american-sig-sauer-assault-rifles-jammu-and-kashmir-1627274-2019-12-11
5. Siddiqui, H. (2020, September 28). India fast tracks procurement of 72,000 assault rifles for the Indian Army. Retrieved from Financial Express: https://www.financialexpress.com/defence/india-fast-tracks-procurement-of-72000-assault-rifles-for-the-indian-army/2093525/
6. Ibid
7. Gurung, S. K. (2020, March 19). Defence Ministry signs contract for 16,479 Light Machine Guns for frontline troops with Israel Weapons Industries. Retrieved from The Economic Times: https://economictimes.indiatimes.com/news/defence/defence-ministry-signs-contract-for-16479-light-machine-guns-for-frontline-troops-with-israel-weapons-industries/articleshow/74716149.cms?from=mdr
8. PTI. (2018, July 15). DRDO hands over tech to defence firm to manufacture bullet-proof jackets. Retrieved from The Economic Times: https://economictimes.indiatimes.com/news/defence/drdo-hands-over-tech-to-defence-firm-to-manufacture-bullet-proof-jackets/articleshow/60944235.cms?from=mdr
9. Peri, D. (2020, July 14). Army to place repeat order for Spike missiles from Israel. Retrieved from The Hindu: https://www.thehindu.com/news/national/army-to-place-repeat-order-for-spike-missiles-from-israel/article32083307.ece
10. Peri, D. (2020, July 12). The Hindu Explains | How is India building up the squadron strength of its air force? Retrieved from The Hindu: https://www.thehindu.com/news/national/the-hindu-explains-how-is-india-building-up-the-squadron-strength-of-its-air-force/article32053910.ece
11. Ibid
12. DNA Web Team. (2020, October 9). DNA Explained: Why ACM AKS Bhadauria said Indian Air Force is ready for two-front war against China, Pakistan. Retrieved from DNA: https://www.dnaindia.com/india/report-dna-explained-why-acm-aks-bhadauria-said-indian-air-force-is-ready-for-a-two-front-war-against-china-and-pakistan-2848629
13. Chand, L. (2020, January). Navy's Quest for Modernisation. Retrieved from SP's Naval Forces: http://www.spsnavalforces.com/story/?id=652&h=Navyandrsquo;s-Quest-for-Modernisation
14. The Economic Times. (2020, March 6). Battle tanks, fighter jets are becoming outdated in modern era: Indian Army Chief. Retrieved from The Economic Times: https://economictimes.indiatimes.com/news/defence/battle-tanks-fighter-jets-are-becoming-outdated-in-modern-era-army-chief/articleshow/74489106.cms\
15. Pandit, R. (2020, August 25). Indian armed forces need to invest in disruptive technologies: Gen Naravane. Retrieved from The Times of India: https://timesofindia.indiatimes.com/india/indian-armed-forces-need-to-invest-in-disruptive-technologies-gen-naravane/articleshow/77744148.cms
16. Ibid
17. Gady, F. S. (2019, September 25). Ajai Shukla on the Current and Future State of India's Military. Retrieved from The Diplomat: https://thediplomat.com/2019/09/ajai-shukla-on-the-current-and-future-state-of-indias-military/

18. Hindustan Times. (2020, August 14). Five things you need to know about Chief of Defence Staff. Retrieved from Hindustan Times: https://www.hindustantimes.com/india-news/five-things-you-need-to-know-about-chief-of-defence-staff/story-2skdaVQwM2YiJqq6D6RX9K.html#:~:text=General%20Bipin%20Rawat%20will%20take,related%20to%20the%20tri%2Dservices.
19. Dutta, A. N. (2019, November 26). Indian Army's new Integrated Battle Groups to be introduced in early 2020. Retrieved from The Print: https://theprint.in/defence/indian-armys-new-integrated-battle-groups-to-be-introduced-in-early-2020/326253/
20. The Economic Times. (2020, October 13). Experts debate the necessity of second Mountain Strike Corps for China border. Retrieved from The Economic Times: https://economictimes.indiatimes.com/news/defence/experts-debate-the-necessity-of-second-mountain-strike-corps-for-china-border/articleshow/78638401.cms
21. Dutta, A. N. (2019, November 26). Indian Army's new Integrated Battle Groups to be introduced in early 2020. Retrieved from The Print: https://theprint.in/defence/indian-armys-new-integrated-battle-groups-to-be-introduced-in-early-2020/326253/
22. Gupta, S. (2020, October 27). India to get 5 military theatre commands, one each for China and Pak. Retrieved from Hindustan Times: https://www.hindustantimes.com/india-news/india-to-get-5-military-theatre-commands-one-each-for-china-and-pak/story-UzFJNollsvpj3tcUetWVNM.html
23. Dhanoa, B. S. (2020, June 30). National security, military modernisation and budgets. Retrieved from Observer Research Foundation: https://www.orfonline.org/expert-speak/national-security-military-modernisation-and-budgets-68775/
24. Singh, R. (2020, August 12). Two HAL light combat choppers deployed in Ladakh. Retrieved from Hindustan Times: https://www.hindustantimes.com/india-news/two-hal-light-combat-choppers-deployed-in-ladakh/story-mQ3MtbvOn9KoNQprZtZw6O.html
25. Katoch, L. C. (2020, June 6). Upgraded Infantry Combat Vehicle 'Sarath'. Retrieved from SP's MAI: http://www.spsmai.com/experts-speak/?id=846&q=Upgraded-Infantry-Combat-Vehicle-Sarath
26. The Economic Times. (2020, October 13). Experts debate the necessity of second Mountain Strike Corps for China border. Retrieved from The Economic Times: https://economictimes.indiatimes.com/news/defence/experts-debate-the-necessity-of-second-mountain-strike-corps-for-china-border/articleshow/78638401.cms
27. Ibid.

5

Defence Procurement

Modernization is a key objective to secure India from rising security threats that lie on either side of its boundaries. Today security threats extend far beyond those emanating from the possibility of conventional warfare, but also have the added dimension of nuclear warfare, network-centric warfare, terrorism, extremism, and cyber warfare. To adequately face these challenges all three branches of the Indian armed forces must be adequately armed and skilled with weapons, systems, and the technical knowhow to resolve evolving threats. However, significant challenges remain ahead of the Ministry of Defence and the three-armed forces which handle matters of procurement, given a history of disjointed planning and budget constraints. With changing political and technical necessities, the nature of procurement has shifted as well. Today's banner of "Make in India" extends to include indigenous production and procurement of military necessities. To make this possible within the constraints of planning and budgeting, India will need to establish an efficient, clear-cut, and cost-effective procurement procedure. Before understanding what such a procurement procedure may look like, a thorough understanding of key factors must be undertaken. These factors include budgeting for procurement, items to procure, and government priorities.

Existing Government Structure for Procurement

The bureaucratic structures around the procurement process primarily involve the Ministry of Defence, the various services, and the DRDO. Within these structures the acquisition process is further handled by the Defence Acquisition Council, Defence Procurement Board, and the Office of Acquisitions. The MoD also produces the Defence Acquisition Procedure (DAP), previously called the Defence Procurement Procedure (DPP), that outlines detailed instructions on how the organization and its acquisition-oriented bodies are to source weapons. The DAP has been a crucial element in inducing efficiency, order, and transparency into the procurement process since its inception in 2002 following the recommendation by the report of the Group of Ministers in 2001. Today, acquisition under these institutions follow certain key priorities and policy objectives. One key element is military modernization and increasing self-reliance. While there have been improvements in domestic capacity to produce weapons, systems, parts, etc., significantly building on these improvements remains a key objective for the Indian defence architecture. There is also a need to build capacity for network centricity, information warfare, and other potential emerging threats such as space warfare. These are areas where India crucially lags behind its allies and rivals.

Red-Tape and its Impact on Procurement

After the 2001 GoM report, several changes have been in the procurement process to streamline and fasten it. This crucially also includes the introduction of a "fast-track" route for acquisition. However, much is left to be done given that India continues to struggle with slow acquisition, tight budget, stifling bureaucracy, and limited self-reliance. Over time, delays and poor planning have actually costed the Ministry of Defence's acquisition plans. For instance, the Indian Air Force has repeatedly tried to acquire the Airbus A330 tanker transport only to withdraw its proposal due to delays and cost constraints[1]. Similarly, the IAF's proposals to buy the Boeing KC-46A were cancelled due to budgetary issues, with the most recent plan only allowing for leasing the aircraft instead of purchasing it. These instances hint at severe issues with adequately planning and budgeting for future procurement needs[2]. The timeline of acquiring a new system is sometimes so long, as illustrated by the above examples, that costs inflate significantly over time posing doubts on the economic viability of the procurement in the first place.

In such cases it also becomes important to consider if technology will remain viable over the period of procurement. This is particularly true given that the evolution of threats and solutions in the case of cyber security is often break-neck and even a delay of a few years may make the procured technology ineffective in the face of the rapidly evolving cyber security threat. This is true not only for procured technologies, but also for administrative bodies that plan for defense procurement and strategy. The Defence Planning Committee, which was created to facilitate indigenous development and create comprehensive defence strategy plans and defence capabilities plans, is now being referred to as "too much too late"[3] as its various committees failed to mitigate the seemingly ad-hoc nature of procurement. Additionally, given that much of these functions will now be overseen by the newly appointed Chief of Defence Staff (CDS), the exact role of the planning committee is unclear as well.

Given the nature of tasks the CDS is to perform, it also likely that the creation of the position will also serve to integrate the procurement needs of the three services. This would be a much needed step in the right direction. For a long time now, the Army, Navy, and the Air Force have been running their procurement operations parallel to each other, with the focus being on ensuring that each force is fully capable of operating alone without support from the other services. Given this, procurement for each service has largely been disjointed from the others[4]. Of course, there is benefit to ensuring that each service has the flexibility to ascertain their own needs and procure what is deemed most necessary. However, given the growing emphasis on network centric warfare and theaterization that requires connectivity and fluid operation between and among the three services, and the central government's plans to create further centralized structures of military governance through the creation of the post of CDS, it is clear the establishment hopes to change the current disjointed nature of procurement. Nonetheless, while intensions are headed in the right direction, neither the CDS nor the MoD has been successful in outlining a plan that is created for the defence establishment rather than the individual services. Thus, this should be a priority for the Indian government as it advances with its efforts towards defense procurement and modernization.

Indigenous Production and Development - "Make in India"

As mentioned earlier, indigenous production under the Make in India banner forms another important pillar of the procurement agenda. Indigenous production is a key step to ensuring that the Indian Armed Forces can remain self-reliant in the long run. Currently, the government relies heavily on foreign partners to source its defence needs. This has costs attached to it. While external partners have their value, these partners are nonetheless sovereign actors who will attempt to create maximum profit from defense dealings and establish leverage for their own governments. In the realm of information warfare relying on foreign software, equipment, servers, etc., can provide added concerns around the security of such acquisitions given fears of malware. Thus, the focus on self-reliance must be emphasized not only conventional fronts, but across the spectrum of cyber warfare, electronic warfare, and space warfare as well.

To support the development of Indigenous solutions to some of these issues, the government operates nine public sector defence entities, like the Hindustan Aeronautics limited and the Bharat Electronics Limited, that have helped in the construction and maintenance of indigenous procurement. The government is also slowly opening itself up to the private sectors to fasten innovation. Of course, the Defence Research and Development Organization (DRDO) and the Ordinance Factory Board (OFB) continue to serve as key state-run institutions to promote indigenous development and production. Despite the presence of these organizations, one report states that the Indian defence industry continues to suffer from mismanagement and poor estimations of cost[5].

In addition to the above-mentioned issues, domestic manufacturing and development is struggling due to serious bureaucracy, with red tape slowing down the process of designing, finding private sector partners, and actualizing production of domestically developed systems. The indigenously developed Battlefield Management System (BMS) and the Infantry Combat Vehicle (ICV) stand as examples of this. First proposed in 2000 as a combat management system to aid network centric warfare capabilities, the BMS is yet to materialize due to tight funding and repeated delays in finalizing design and prototyping. The ICV has similarly suffered from constant setbacks while choosing private sector partners and developing prototypes. However, it is important to note that the Indian private sector has shown that is possess the knowhow and ability to design and produce such systems. Therefore, it is upon the government to ensure that it's able to provide enough incentives for such organizations to respond to government requests by instilling mechanisms that shorten lengthy time frames and reduce red tape.

Budgetary Constraints

Budgetary issues, while they have been featured earlier, deserve a deeper consideration. As has been mentioned, lack of funding is a reoccurring hurdle to allowing for ease in acquisitions and military modernization. SIPRI states that given the current defence budget of $71.1 billion, a 6.8% increase relative to 2018, India is now the third highest military spender in the world, after the US and China[6]. Of this amount, the most significant increase in funds has been directed towards facilitating greater pensions and salaries for servicemen. However, even with this increase in allocation, the Indian military is far from receiving adequate funding. One MoD official stated that the overall increase in funds was not even sufficient to cover for inflation costs[7]. The MoD's estimates of required funds have repeatedly stood in stark contrast to what the Ministry of Finance has been able to provide. Amit Cowshish[8], former financial advisor (Acquisitions), highlights that the 11th five year defence plan was halted in its tracks primarily due to the MoF's inability to allocate the quantity of funds planners in the Ministry of Defence envisioned. In 2012, the MoD did not even approach the MoF to seek consent on the subsequent 12th five-year plan. Following this, the Defence Planning Committee was created to smooth out such issues in the future. However, as was highlighted above the committee itself has been largely ineffective and may now be moot given the presence of newer centralized structures.

In terms of the impact the most recent budget has had on procurement procedures, all three service have suffered from setbacks. A key issue in terms of planning for big-ticket or small-ticket items in this scenario is the volatile nature of budget allocations themselves. For the purchase of bid-ticket equipment for instance, multiyear planning that is supported by the assurance that funding would be secure across the duration of the procurement timeline is required. Yet, the defense budget itself is released on a yearly basis, forcing the services to re-contemplate procurement plans yearly as well. This inevitably forces the services to function in the short term even if they have detailed procurement plans for the long term laid out. For instance, the Navy had to cancel plans to procure 24 MH-60R multirole helicopters from the United States due to insufficient funds after this year's budget was provided. Similarly, the Indian Army and the Indian Air Force had to limit their initial procurement plans as well[9]. Finally, given the ongoing pandemic, it is likely these budgeting issues will only exacerbate as the government shifts funding to other sectors such social welfare and economic relief bills.

Recommendations

Given the state of the defence acquisition processes as it stands, it is clear that much needs to change in terms of long-term planning mechanisms, resource allocation, and indigenous production. The current structures that handle procurement are numerous and the system is far from smooth and efficient. While the DPS largely failed to induce many reforms in procurement planning or streamline the procurement process, the new Chief of Defence Staff may be able to bring about these changes. While, it stands to reason that the individual services will have the most intimate understand of what equipment is needed; a joint effort between all three forces must be made to outline how to pursue their procurement goals collectively in a way that aids India's national security in the long term. To this end, the office of the CDS can play a critical role.

As has been mentioned, long-term planning in and of itself, while having occurred on paper, is still a distant dream. India must step away from its tendency to set short term budget allocations for its defence complex that make them vulnerable to the vagaries of economy. This is particularly important given that procurement processes, for better or for worse, tends to take years on end and annual uncertainties around budgets certainly doesn't help speed the process up. Such long-term planning, Laxman Kumar Bahera[10] states, is only possible with the creation of a national security strategy that outlines India's long-term national security vision and direction. The presence of a forward looking national white paper or strategy document will not only lend credence to the MoD's long-term procurement plans, it would also provide it direction. Depending on what such a document would highlight as key areas of investment, procurement of equipment needed to augment cyber, space, information, or network centric warfare capabilities could gain further credence and receive more impetus. However, this is likely to remain out of reach given that such a document has long been absent from the defence circle despite repeated efforts by the DPC. The newly created CDS may be the change needed to push such a step forward. However, if all else fails, then perhaps one could revisit the 2001 GoM's report that advised for the creation of a sperate body for defence related acquisitions that would not be bogged down by additional functions and would provide a single agency that can be held accountable for flaws in the procurement system.

The Indian government, together with the Ministry of Finance and other relevant ministries, must also work to outline multi-year budgets for defence needs. If there are concerns that such a fixed plan will unfeasibly lock in the Indian government into unaffordable deals, then perhaps another solution could be conceived. For instance, one solution might be to make a part of the budget fixed for the long-term, while keeping another quantity open to fluctuations on a yearly basis to allow the government more flexibility to change the allocation of funds based on changing needs. India can also reduce regulation and red tape that may be disincentivizing private organizations from engaging with defence related manufacturing contracts. Time delays and escalated costs are also a product of bureaucratic shortfalls. While the DAP sets up details guidelines on procurement procedures, delays due around drawing up plans, conducting biddings for choosing private sector partners, and then working with these partners to develop systems contribute to bloating the cost of procurement and often force the ministry to pay prices over the budget or drop the project entirely. These issues must be targeted in future versions of the DAP or other procurement plans.

The above-mentioned changes would also help bolster the Make in India initiative by allowing for easier private sector participation and more timely and steadier funding. However, the current scope of indigenously created equipment must grow in scope and quality. In addition to big ticket projects such as the creation of indigenous tanks, submarines, ships, torpedoes, etc., domestic production of parts and other equipment must be made a central focus as well. Currently, India suffers from a deficiency in parts in addition to an aging armoury of weapons. In addition to this, procurement of combat gear, other than weapons, is also dependent on international partners even though

India has the manufacturing capacity to produce it domestically[11]. This is an area that requires further investment on the part of the Indian government and the Ministry of Defence. Afterall, dedicating funding overwhelmingly to major weapons purchases, without the supporting spare parts or equipment is a short-sighted investment.

Finally, while indigenous development must remain a key pillar of procurement for India, foreign procurement must not be entirely phased out. Instead, foreign sources can be crucial in speeding India's slow progress by helping build up an inventory of disposable spares by collaborating with those states that are using similar platforms as India. They can also be of help sourcing key technologies that the domestic manufacturers are far from being able to develop indigenously at competitive prices. Thus, rather than targeting for full indigenization at the earliest, it would be more economical to focus resources set for 'make in India' to only specific high priority sectors. This way, financial resources are not spread too thin, while Indian manufacturers can focus on producing defence equipment that they have a proven ability to produce at the highest quality. Maintaining diplomatic connections in this way also helps in maintaining India's strategic partnerships with key allies who can, in turn, provide India with the technical assistance to support research and development.

Notes

1. The Week. (2019, October 04). IAF hunts for aerial refuellers again: A saga of cancelled deals. Retrieved from: https://www.theweek.in/news/india/2019/10/04/hunt-for-aerial-refuellers-another-never-ending-saga-for-iaf.html
2. Singh, R. (2020, March 23). Indian Air Force may lease aerial refuelling tanker craft. Retrieved from the Hindustan Times: https://www.hindustantimes.com/india-news/indian-air-force-may-lease-aerial-refuelling-tanker-craft/story-8RzD9OwZs7M0Hc9wM5KzJP.html
3. Bhaskar, C.U. (2018, April 19). Defence Planning Committee: Is too much being attempted too late?. Retrieved from the Hindustan Times: https://www.hindustantimes.com/opinion/defence-planning-committee-is-too-much-being-attempted-too-late/story-vex9VpaqIW57kasE3c6YRI.html
4. Behera, L. K. (2012, March). India's Defence Acquisition System: Need for Further Reforms. The Korean Journal of Defense Analysis. 24(1). Retrieved from: http://kida.re.kr/data/kjda/06_Laxman_Kumar_Behera.pdf
5. Das, P. (2020, April 15). India's defence procurement policy 2020: Old wine in a new bottle. Retrieved from the Observer Research Foundation: https://www.orfonline.org/expert-speak/indias-defence-procurement-policy-2020-old-wine-in-a-new-bottle-64673/#:~:text=The%20Ministry%20of%20Defence%20(MoD,%E2%80%9CMake%20in%20India%E2%80%9D%20initiative.
6. SIPRI. (2020, April 27). Global military expenditure sees largest annual increase in a decade – says SIPRI – reaching $1917 billion in 2019. Retrieved from the

Stockholm International Peace Research Institute: https://www.sipri.org/media/press-release/2020/global-military-expenditure-sees-largest-annual-increase-decade-says-sipri-reaching-1917-billion#:~:text=China's%20military%20expenditure%20reached%20%24261,spending%2C'%20says%20Siemon%20T.

7. Raghuvanshi, V. (2020, February 04). New weapons purchases suffer under India's defence budget. Retrieved from Defence News: https://www.defensenews.com/global/asia-pacific/2020/02/04/new-weapons-purchases-suffer-under-indias-latest-defense-budget/
8. Cowshish, A. (2020, August 24). It Is Time to Accept That India's Defence Planning is Crippled by Severe Financial Woes. Retrieved from The Wire: https://thewire.in/security/india-defence-planning-procurement-finance-ministry
9. Raghuvanshi, V. (2020, February 04). New weapons purchases suffer under India's defence budget. Retrieved from Defence News: https://www.defensenews.com/global/asia-pacific/2020/02/04/new-weapons-purchases-suffer-under-indias-latest-defense-budget/
10. Behera, L. K. (2012, March). India's Defence Acquisition System: Need for Further Reforms. The Korean Journal of Defense Analysis. 24(1). Retrieved from: http://kida.re.kr/data/kjda/06_Laxman_Kumar_Behera.pdf
11. Bedi, R. (2020, August 09). Despite Advances in Strategic Arms, Country Fails 'Make in India' test for Basic Equipment. Retrieved from: https://thewire.in/security/make-in-india-strategic-arms-import-defence-industrial-base

6

Police and Paramilitary Management

Apart from the many external threats that the Republic faces in contemporary times, is the threat that India faces from elements within our borders. The Indian Army, Air Force and Navy (and Coast Guard, among other branches) have been combatting the external threats that attempt at disturbing harmonious sovereignty of the state and people, imposing their deviant interests through all means regardless of the political morality, of said means. At the same time, the Government has also been engaged, since the birth of the Republic, in combatting the many instances of internal threats, elements and organisations propagating violence of political nature against the Indian state and people.

As has also been highlighted above, one such instance of an internal threat that the nation faces today can be seen deep inside the hinterlands of central-eastern India, in states such as Jharkhand, Chhattisgarh, Orissa and West Bengal where left-wing extremism finds a fertile breeding ground. The Maoist-Naxal insurgency has had a lot of history, from 1947 in modern-day Telangana to 1967 in West Bengal. The modern edition, which is relevant today, dates back to a surge of violence and insurgency in 2004. While the insurgency has been battered down, Maoist violence against the state continues to remain a threat. On March 21, 2020, 17 troopers of the Central Reserve Police Force, India's premier paramilitary force, were killed in action in a Maoist ambush in Sukma, Chhattisgarh. On May 1, 2019, another Maoist ambush led to the deaths of 16 officers of the State Police in Gadchiroli, Maharashtra. On April 24, 2017, 26 troopers of the CRPF were killed in action in Sukma, Chhattisgarh, after the 99-strong government forces were ambushed by around 300 Maoist terrorists. There have been many more such attacks. As per data released by the Ministry of Home Affairs to the Lok Sabha, the following events took place between the years 1999 and 2016[1]:

- 26,511 incidents involving left-wing extremist elements took place in the country
- 7,615 civilians were killed as part of these incidents

- 2,585 personnel of Indian security forces were killed in action
- 3,019 Maoist-Naxalite-terrorists were eliminated
- A total death toll of 13,219 killed was reported between 1999-2016 as part of left-wing extremism in India

Some of the groups involved in the Maoist- Naxalite conflict include[2]:

- Communist Party of India – Maoist (CPI-M)
- People's Liberation Guerrilla Army (PLGA; armed wing of CPI-M)
- Communist Party of United States of India
- People's War Group (PWG)
- People's Liberation Army of Manipur (PLAMP)
- Akhil Bharat Nepali Ekta Samaj (ABNES)
- Maoist Communist Party of Manipur (MCMP)
- Kangleipak Communist Party (KCP)
- Tamil Nadu Liberation Army (TNLA)

The unity of the Republic is also faced with the threat of secession and separatists in the volatile North-eastern states of the country. There are multiple armed separatist organisations and factions that are currently active in the region. Most of these organisations propagate the establishment of independent states by seceding from the Republic of India. Other groups will settle for the establishment of regional autonomy within the Union, creating an atmosphere of legal duality with the application of a separate set of laws and norms.

Assam has, historically, been a state which has faced a lot of heat due to the militancy of the Northeast. Geography can have said to have played a detrimental factor, regarding militancy and cross-border violence. Assam is centrally located in the region, having borders with all states: Arunachal Pradesh, Nagaland, Manipur, Mizoram, Tripura, Meghalaya and with West Bengal. This means that extremists and their causes tend to spill over into Assamese borders, in addition to other such elements already operating within state boundaries. Further on, the Assamese have had historically porous borders with neighbouring countries Bangladesh and Bhutan. The illegal movement of extremist elements and illegal migrants adds on to the state government's plate of issues. Similar movement across the dodgy Indo-Myanmarese border could further add on to the problems of the Assamese authorities. The state of Assam has had its own domestic terror groups as well, much of which propagated secessionism and separatism. These groups, including names such as The United Liberation Front of Assam, National Democratic Front of Bodoland, Kamtapur Liberation Organisation, et cetera, are mostly defunct today.

Nagaland was carved out of Assam in 1963. However, since before it was even established as an individual state of the Union, the Naga people were engaged in a secessionist cause to establish a state independent from New Delhi. Groups such as the Naga National Council and the National Socialist Council of Nagaland were set up to stir chaos and violence in a bid to further the cause of secession. Members of guerrilla groups such as the Naga Federal Army are also said to have received training and equipment support from Beijing. In 2015, the Modi administration signed a landmark peace agreement with the National Socialist Council of Nagaland, thereby concluding a conflict that went on for over six decades. "The government recognized the unique history, culture and position of the Nagas and their sentiments and aspirations. The NSCN understood and appreciated the Indian political system and governance"[3]. Thuingaleng Muivah, leader of the NSCN-IM faction, who signed the accord in presence of PM Narendra Modi at a function at 7 Lok Kalyan Marg, later issued a written statement saying:

> *"A better understanding has been arrived at and a framework agreement has been concluded basing on the unique history and position of the Nagas and recognising the universal principle that in a democracy, sovereignty lies with the people."*[4]

Manipur formally joined the Union of India in 1949, a move which by rebels and secessionists was portrayed as an involuntary one by a powerless state. In 1972, Manipur was formally established as an individual state, which did not quench the hunger of the separatist groups and movement fuelling the violence within the state. As a result, the state has been under the jurisdiction of the Armed Forces Special Powers Act of 1958 since 1980. As of today, 12 insurgent groups are said to be active in the state[5]:

- Kangleipak Communist Party (KCP)
- Kanglei Yawol Kanna Lup (KYKL)
- Manipur People's Liberation Front (MPLF)
- People's Revolutionary Party of Kangleipak (PREPAK)
- People's Liberation Army (PLA)
- United National Liberation Front (UNLF)
- Coordination Committee (CorCom)
    - Kangleipak Communist Party (KCP)
    - Kanglei Yawol Kanna Lup (KYKL)
    - People's Revolutionary Party of Kangleipak
    - Revolutionary People's Front
    - United National Liberation Front (UNLF)
    - United Peoples Party of Kangleipak (UPPK)
- Manipur Naga Revolutionary Front (MNRF)
- National Socialist Council of Nagaland
    - Isak-Muivah faction (NSCN-IM)
    - Khaplang faction (NSCN-K)
- People's United Liberation Front (PULF)
- Zeliangrong United Front (ZUF).

In March 2020, the Union Minister of State for Home Affairs – G Kishan Reddy – informed the Rajya Sabha that the Northeast had witnessed a 70 per cent reduction in insurgency incidents, 78 per cent reduction in security forces casualties and an 80 per cent drop in civilian deaths in 2019, compared to the situation in 2013. Several memorandums and understandings have been reached between the Central & State Governments and militant groups in the region. However, it is important also to note the casualties incurred over records of violence spread over two decades between 1999-2019[6]:

- 10,314 civilians were killed as part of violence in the Northeast
- 2,767 personnel of Indian security forces were killed in action
- 8,554 terrorists were eliminated
- A total death toll of 21,635 killed was reported in the given time frame

The conflict in Kashmir is a mix of internal as well as external actors and factors fuelling a tremendous degree of chaos, turmoil and loss of life and property. The British exit from the Indian sub-continent did not end with a pretty sight. What generations had dreamt of and generations had fought for left the former colony gave way for the formation of two new states divided by spilt blood. What emerged from this mess was a constitutional Republic of India and the Islamic Republic of Pakistan. The two states entered a state of war in 1947 when the Pakistanis, having employed non-regular, tribal fighters invaded the newly drawn yet porous borders of India in Jammu & Kashmir. In response, India was quick to airlift troops and equipment from New Delhi to Srinagar. The war lasted 14 months and ended with a United Nations-sponsored ceasefire and the formulation of the Line of Control which established a de facto Pakistani-occupied territory in the Indian state of Jammu & Kashmir.

The war ended in 1948, but the conflict is being fought to this day. Several wars and skirmishes have been fought since then. While India has won all confrontations against the Pakistani enemy, victory has come at too high a cost for it to be called affordable. The Pakistanis have tapped the vulnerability of the people of the Kashmir valley. The Pakistanis have also, since 1947, actively employed irregular forces (such as *lashkars*) for furthering their interests in the disputed territory. The services of irregulars and tribal fighters were employed in 1947, 1965 as well as in 1999. The irregulars have been on multiple occasions, both in the past and present, been used to incite radicalism, extremism, religious fundamentalism and to spark violence in the Indian border state. In 1989, with the withdrawal of Soviet forces from Afghanistan, a massive surge of violence was felt in Jammu & Kashmir with the killings and forced exodus of Kashmiri Pandits – a Hindu-minority community in a Muslim-majority region. At this time, thousands of Kashmiri youth moved across the Indo-Pakistani borders to receive militant training and equipment, only to return to Kashmir to further a Pakistani-backed agenda of breaking the sovereign

Indian state away from the Union. Several groups have played a fundamental role in the valley. This includes[7]:

- Hizbul-Mujahideen
- Harkat-ul Mujahideen
- Lashkar-e-Taiba
- Jaish-e-Mohammed
- Al-Badr
- Jamiat-ul-Mujahideen
- Harkat-ul-Jehad-al-Islami
- Al-Umar Mujahideen
- Dukhtaran-e-Millat
- Lashkar-e-Omar
- Lashkar-e-Jabbar
- Tehrik-ul-Mujahideen
- Jammu & Kashmir Liberation Front
- All Parties Hurriyat Conference
- Mutahida Jehad Council
- Al Qaeda in Indian Subcontinent
- Islamic State of Iraq and Syria – Khorasan Province

The violence which surged in the 1990s claimed thousands of lives and called upon extremists to commit unimaginable atrocities against harmless innocents. In this, the government failed to prevent the loss of life. The numbers recorded in the time frame 1990-2017 by sources in the Ministry of Home Affairs are nought if not truly horrifying[8]:

- 22,794 incidents involving radicalism/terrorism/religious fundamentalism took place
- 13,979 civilians were killed as part of violence in Jammu and Kashmir
- 5,131 personnel of Indian security forces were killed in action
- 25,457 terrorists were eliminated
- A total death toll of 44,567 killed was reported in the given time frame

The Central Armed Police Forces

The Ministry of Home Affairs as established by the Constitution of the Republic of India is entrusted with the preservation of internal security, border management, the administration of healthy Centre-State relations, administration of Union Territories, management of Central Armed Police Forces, disaster management, et cetera. In pursuance of these obligations, the Ministry of Home Affairs continuously monitors the internal security situation, issues appropriate advisories, shares intelligence inputs, extends manpower and financial support, guidance and expertise to the state governments for maintenance of security, peace and harmony without encroaching upon the constitutional rights of the states[9].

For the context of this study, the Ministry of Home Affairs' responsibilities of preserving internal security of the state and the management of its long and volatile borders will be of prime importance. The concerned departments of the Ministry are the Department of Border Management and the Department of Internal Security.

The Department of Internal Security handles the Indian Police Service, internal security and law & order, insurgency, terrorism, naxalism, activities of inimical foreign agencies, terrorist financing, rehabilitation, the grant of visa and other immigration matters. It is this department that overwatches the conduct of duties of India's many Central Armed Police Forces. The CAPF include five major branches discussed ahead.

Central Reserve Police Force

The CRPF is the largest of the CAPFs, having entered into existence in 1949 with the rechristening of the colonial-era Crown Representative's Police, under the CRPF Act of the same year. Since then, it has become the premier central police force of the state. It has served the Indian nation in all ways possible, by assisting in the defence of the state against Chinese and Pakistani Aggression, in rooting the Maoist-Naxalite threat the hinterlands of the country faces, as well as ensuring the preservation of law & order during the sensitive turn of events, such as riots. Other duties performed by the CRPF include Crowd control, counter militancy, participating in United Nations Peace Keeping missions as per government policy, rescue and relief operations at the time of natural calamities and disasters, fighting enemies at the time of war and the overall coordination of large-scale security arrangement especially with regard to elections in disturbed areas.

In the 81 years of its history, the CRPF has grown into the largest of India's central police forces, with 246 Battalions size strength[10]:

- 208 Executive Battalions
- 6 Mahila Battalions
- 15 Rapid Action Force Battalions
- 10 CoBRA (Commando Battalion for Resolute Action) Battalions
- 5 Signal Battalions
- 1 Special Duty Group
- 1 Parliament Duty Group

After the nation attained its independence from its colonial history, several contingents of the CRPF were deployed in sensitive areas along the Indo-Pak border, at Kutch, in Rajasthan and also in Jammu & Kashmir. The CRPF bore the brunt of the first Chinese attack on India at Hot Springs, Ladakh in 1959, when a small CRPF patrol party was ambushed by the People's Liberation Army in which ten of its men were killed in action. The CRPF also assisted the Indian Army in Arunachal Pradesh in the first Indo-China war of 1962. Since then, the CRPF has been actively deployed across the vast terrain of this country. The CRPF is the prime security force dealing with the threats of the Naxalites in Central-East India. The force also plays an active role in combatting rebels and maintaining tranquillity in the seven sister's region, ensuring that all corners of the nation remain connected to one another and may not face any scenarios of deprivation of goods, services and resources.

Central Industrial Security Force

The CISF is the prime central police force that safeguards the security of over 300 industrial units, government infrastructure projects & facilities and establishments located all over the country. The force came into existence in 1969, to provide integrated security cover to the Public Sector Undertakings (PSUs) which, in those years, occupied the commanding heights of the economy. With globalization and liberalization of the economy, CISF is no longer a PSU-centric organization. Instead, it has become a premier multi-skilled security agency of the country, mandated to provide security to major critical infrastructure installations of the country in diverse areas[11].

CISF is currently providing security cover to strategic establishments, including the Department of Space, the Department of Atomic Energy, Airports, Delhi Metro, seaports, power-plants, sensitive Government institutions and buildings, historical monuments as well as basic areas of Indian economic apparatus such as petroleum, natural gas, electricity, coal, steel and mining facilities[12]. As of today, the CISF operates 12 Battalions, 8 training institutes and 63 other formations. The mandated size of the police force was raised to 141,421 personnel as of March 1, 2020.

Border Security Force

The BSF is India's first line of defence and the primary border security organisation. It was established post the Indo-Pak war in 1965 for ensuring the security of the borders of India and for matters connected therewith. Until then, the international borders of the country were manned and guarded by individual states' armed police battalions. The Border Security Force was born with the mandate of guarding India's borders with Pakistan, which in 1965, still ruled over Bangladesh, formerly East Pakistan. Therefore, the BSF today guards not only the explosive border with Pakistan but also the porous border with Bangladesh.

During times of peace, the BSF is tasked with the prevention of trans-national/border criminal activity, unauthorised entry and/or exit from Indian territory and the prevention of smuggling and other illegal activities. During times of war, the roles of the BSF evolve into more complex and extensive ones. The mandate includes and is not limited to[13]:

- Holding ground in less threatened sectors so long as the main attack does not develop in a particular sector and it is felt that the local situation is within the capability of BSF to deal with. The BSF units can continue to remain deployed in the particular sector even in a war situation to release the Army for offensive tasks. In the event of a major attack developing, which is not within the capacity of the BSF to deal with, the Army can be expected to either reinforce the BSF with artillery or other support or relieve the BSF from its role in the particular sector.
- Protection of vital installations particular airfields against enemy commandoes/paratroopers or raids. The role can be entrusted to the BSF Units which are placed under the Army's operational control.
- Providing extension to the flanks of the main defence line by the holding of strong points in conjunction with other units.
- Limited aggressive action against paramilitary or irregular forces of the enemy within the overall plan of the armed forces.
- Performing special tasks connected with intelligence including raids. These are tasks which might be entrusted to BSF units by the Army in a war situation according to local necessity. It would, however, be expected that the state of training and equipment of the particular BSF units would be kept in view in assessing their adequacy for the tasks.
- Maintenance of law and order in enemy territory administrated under the control of the Army. Normally, the local civil police force would be utilized for this task but the BSF could be used to supplement the civil police or to act in lieu thereof in a situation where civil police are not readily available.
- Guarding of prisoners of war camps and cages.
- Assistance in control of refugees. It is the intention to use civil police force and armed home guards etc. for these tasks but again depending upon local exigencies, the BSF might be entrusted with these tasks.
- Anti-infiltration duties in assigned areas. This is an important responsibility which will have to be performed by security forces. The exact responsibility of the BSF in this matter is still under consideration and separate instructions are expected to be issued.

The Border Security Force also regularly contributes to Peace Keeping Missions of the United Nations. The force also takes part in rescue and relief operations in areas struck by natural disasters and calamities.

Indo-Tibetan Border Police

The ITBP was born after the Chinese invasion of territories along the northern frontier in the Indo-China war of 1962. The war saw India lose jurisdiction over the disputed Aksai Chin region of Ladakh, which continues to remain occupied by the People's Liberation Army today. The force was tasked with reorganizing the frontier defence apparatus, setting up intelligence-gathering networks and ensuring the physical security and integrity of the Indo-Tibetan border.

With additional tasks entrusted to ITBP from time to time on border guarding, counter-insurgency and internal security roles, the number of ITBP Battalions increased gradually and ITBP presently has 56 service Battalions, 4 Specialist Battalions, 17 Training Centres and 07 logistics establishments with a total strength of approx. 90,000 personnel[14]. Eventually, in 2004, the ITBP was given jurisdiction over the manning of the entirety of the Indo-China border, as part of the 'One Border One Force' decree. ITBP replaced Assam Rifles, which had earlier guarded the Indo-China border along with the states of Sikkim and Arunachal Pradesh.

The ITBP has also begun to take on several other tasks into its mandate. As per direction from the Ministry of Home Affairs, 8 battalions of the ITBP are currently deployed alongside the CRPF to thwart Maoist-Naxalite threats in Chhattisgarh. The ITBP also takes up roles in guarding various installations of national importance such as the Rashtrapati Bhawan, Vice President House, Rumtek Monastery (Gangtok, Sikkim), Tihar Jail (North Delhi), Lal Bahadur Shastri National Academy of Administration (Charleville, Uttarakhand) and various sensitive installations in Chandigarh (Punjab) & Jammu (J&K). Apart from installation protection, the ITBP can also be charged with the preservation and restoration of law & order in disturbed areas. It also has a highly-trained team deployed to protect the Indian Embassy and its workers in Kabul, along with 4 Consulate Generals of India in Afghanistan, at Herat, Kandahar, Jalalabad and Mazar-e-Sharif. Personnel of the ITBP were also deployed for United Nations Peace Keeping operations in Angola, Namibia, Cambodia, Bosnia & Herzegovina, Mozambique and Kosovo[15].

Assam Rifles

Assam Rifles is the oldest and highest decorated paramilitary force of the Republic of India. The force can trace its origins back to 1835 as the 'Cachar Levy', a small militia-like force mandated with the protection of British tea estates and their settlements against tribal raids. The name changed eventually to Assam Rifles, in 1917, as a recognition of the valour of the organisation which fought shoulder-to-shoulder with the British Army in the Great War of 1914-18.

Running down history lane, the role of the Assam Rifles remained crucial to the preservation of peace, tranquillity and stability in the Northeast. The Assam Rifles has engaged in combatting both internal as well as external threats. It has fought against Chinese aggression in the Northeast sector during 1962, as well as countering insurgency and militancy in the region. The Paramilitary force has also participated in the 1980s Indian intervention – Op Pawan – in Sri Lanka. The Assam Rifles is also tasked with guarding the Indo-Myanmarese border, preventing illegal migration and the activities of transnational criminal syndicates, among other elements.

Today the Force remains deployed in some of the most remote and underdeveloped areas and provides security to locals. Assam Rifles has grown substantially over the years from 17 battalions in 1960 to 46 battalions at present. Through its long deployment in the tribal belt, the Assam Rifles has earned the complete confidence of the locals and has helped considerably in bringing the people of this region into the national mainstream[16]. The 'Sentinels of the Northeast', as they are called, are tasked with the conduct of counter-insurgency operations in the region, and other areas where deemed necessary, under control of the army (AFSPA). During war, the Assam Rifles ensure rear area security in assigned areas. They also act as a penultimate interventionist force of the central government in the internal security situation, under the control of the army, when the situation goes beyond the control of central paramilitary operations. The Assam Rifles have contributed significantly to opening up the Seven Sisters to administration and commerce. It thus came to be known as the 'right arm of the civil and left arm of the military'.

Sashastra Seema Bal(SSB)

The SSB is a border guard force deployed along India's international borders with Bhutan and Nepal. The Central Armed Police Force was founded in the wake of the Indo-China war of 1962 to create a unique, unconventional yet specialized organization, which would function in the far-flung, vulnerable, strategic, remote, climatically and topographically difficult border areas and motivate the border population across several states towards the cause of protecting Indian national sovereignty and integrity of the state. The border guard agency is also the lead intelligence gathering agency for the region, along both Indo-Nepali and Indo-Tibetan borderlands. The Sashastra Seema Bal's present charter of duties is to[17]:

- Safeguard the security of assigned borders of India and promote a sense of security among the people living in border areas.
- Prevent trans-border crimes, smuggling and any other illegal activities.
- Prevent unauthorized entry into or exit from the territory of India.
- Carry out civic action programme in the area of responsibility.
- Perform any other duty assigned by the Central Government. (SSB is being deployed for Law & Order, Counter Insurgency Operations and Election duty)

The 2,450 km long Indo- Nepal and Indo- Bhutan border is more challenging because the open border not only provides alluring encouragement to traffickers and smugglers but, also offers huge opportunities for militants/ ANEs trained on foreign soil to infiltrate and pose a serious threat to national security. It is extremely difficult to seal the entire border effectively owing to its porosity and visa-free regime on one hand and social economic and cultural relationship of bordering countries on the other, but SSB, by virtue of its enormous experience of working at grass root level in remote areas, can muster people's support and cooperation besides physically guarding the border and maintaining its sanctity[18]. The SSB currently commands 73 Battalions with 78,809 personnel in total. It also has 5 battalions deployed in UT Jammu & Kashmir to counter Islamic radicalism and terrorism, and 3 battalions in Bihar, 2 battalions each in Chhattisgarh and Jharkhand to counter left-wing extremism.[19]

Operational Learnings and Drawbacks

The Ministry of Home Affairs has been consistently striving toward the improvement of command and management systems of all branches of the Central Armed Police Forces. Several steps have been taken to improve the capabilities and cooperation of central and state-level intelligence agencies. The Multi-Agency Centre (MAC) and State Multi-Agency Centre (SMAC) are set up to share intelligence gathered by the several units active in the fight against Left Wing Extremism in Central-East India. In furtherance to this conflict, the Joint Command & Control Centre is set up at Jagdalpur, Chhattisgarh and Gaya, Bihar, to improve inter-agency cooperation, among local, state and central law enforcement agencies and strengthening of technical and human intelligence gathered by all levels of intelligence-gathering bureaus and agencies.

In the Northeast, the central and state governments are working hand-in-hand to maintain law & order by curbing unlawful activities by illicit and militant organisations operating in the area. The Armed Forces Special Powers Act of 1958 is currently imposed in the entirety of Assam, Manipur, Nagaland (except Imphal), Districts of Tirap, Changlang and Longding (and areas bordering the state of Assam) in Arunachal Pradesh, and the areas in Meghalaya along its state border with Assam[20]. In this regard, the Central Armed Police Forces work side by side with other security agencies and the Ministry of Home Affairs is pushing for the creation of a unified command structure in the region. New Delhi is also assisting local and state law-enforcement agencies to modernise equipment available to use as well as aiding the training and tactical development of its cadre. In the Union Territory of Jammu & Kashmir, several CAPFs battalions are deployed along-side the J&K Police, the Indian Army, and the Army-led and manned Rashtriya Rifles paramilitary force. While the Army, RR and J&K police conduct major operations in the volatile valley, the main task assigned to the CAPF troopers deployed in the region is to ensure stability and maintain law & order in rear positions. However, CAPFs have also at multiple occasions been deployed to major operations alongside other frontline security agencies when said agencies faced manpower shortage in the immediate area.

The importance of the role of CAPFs as peacekeepers of the nation only caught the eye of the nation in 2010, with the launch of Operation Green Hunt[21] – the Ministry of Home Affairs' campaign to crush the Naxalite threat in the 'red corridor'. However, many strides have been made over the years, the campaign has still not resulted in any decisive or ultimate victory for the government; the red threat remains. This is mostly so due to lack of coordination and cooperation among the several agencies involved in the campaign. The state police take primacy in intelligence and the conduct of operations and have failed to utilise optimally the resources the central government provides, in way of the deployment of CAPFs. Instead of using the CAPFs in focused area operations supporting the state police, they were either idled for lack of operational planning or used for solo operations without the intelligence support of the state police. On most occasions, the overall CAPF deployment hardly matched their operational or developmental requirements, necessitating remedial intervention in strategic deployments by the Ministry of Home Affairs[22].

On April 6, 2010, 75 troopers of the 62nd Battalion of the Central Reserve Police Force were killed in action in what came to be known as the Dantewada massacre. Probes conducted by the Ministry of Home Affairs suggested that the company of CRPF troopers violated standard operating procedures and did not stick to the earmarked patrol task with specific grid references, made its own rules by moving in and around the area where they were finally attacked by the Maoists[23]. Auftragstaktik, or battle-time orders, can make a world of difference on the battlefield and can tip the balance on either side in combat. In this case, the lack of a good sense of leadership and decision-making led to the eventual slaughter of 75 security personnel. Apart from this unfortunate event, the lack of an able leadership to command the CAPFs and to enforce the adherence of its cadres to the standard operating procedures is widespread. Violations include but are not limited to[24]:

- Personnel operating with drained walkie-talkie sets
- Travelling on top of open tractors
- Not using seatbelts and helmets while travelling in landmine proof vehicles
- Not walking in single-file formation
- Using motorbikes during long-range patrolling on non-tarred roads – those most likely to be mined
- Frequently using the same route for operations, thereby making themselves vulnerable to being ambushed

In order to be seen as Peacekeepers of the nation, it is an absolute necessity for the CAPFs to be seen as friends of the civilian population – a helping hand and not soulless trigger-pullers. A majority of the CAPFs deployed anywhere in the country, come from every nook and corner of the country. At times, the security personnel would find it difficult to distinguish the Maoists from tribals and civilians. The forces needed to adopt a typical counterinsurgency approach of 'isolating the fish from the sea' by winning the trust of the civilian population. This means, minimising collateral damage. Once a designated area is cleared of extremist elements, the civil administration of the state and central government needs to move in and provide for the socioeconomic needs and requirements of the local population, to ensure that radicalism and extremism do not find any breeding ground. However, large bureaucracy, systematic corruption and unenthusiastic administrations meant that the financial resources the New Delhi allocated to the freshly liberated hinterlands did not always find their way to their ultimate destination.

In the Northeast, CAPFs face issues similar to those in Central and East India. One of the core problems of these central police forces will always remain that their battalions are comprised of citizens from every corner of the Republic. Like in the 'Red Belt', most CAPFs faced similar challenges in distinguishing tribals from insurgents, as well as unfamiliarity and incompatibility with local terrain and environment. However, in the Northeast, the Assam Rifles plays the key role as the 'Sentinels of the Northeast'. The Assam Rifles have an edge over the other branches of the CAPFs such as the CRPF or the BSF in way of being a historically ever-present paramilitary force, consisting of a sizeable strength of soldiers of local origin and background.

Despite this edge, there have been certain drawbacks in the region. For many years, India was unable to involve neighbouring countries such as Bangladesh, Bhutan and Myanmar in taking an active stance against insurgent elements that operated within Indian borders and were able to take refuge, undetected, in said countries. However, a lot of progress has been made in this regard with the maturity and further development in ties with these countries. Another issue that has been consistent and widespread among all theatres of operations and all branches of India's Central Armed Police Forces has been the issue of modernisation in the field of intelligence gathering apparatus and strategic and tactical capabilities of the leadership. State police forces take primacy in gathering intelligence and decision making.

Lack of coordination with CAPFs and associated agencies tends to bring about a suboptimal decision-making process by the local agencies, as well as having a negative impact on the reciprocal intelligence sharing process. The fact that a section within the police force in states such as Assam, Manipur, and Nagaland had been compromised and for several years-maintained connections with the insurgents, regularly providing them with information regarding planned offensives, largely neutralised the projected gains of CAPF operations. Inter-ministerial and bureaucratic clashes between the Ministry of Home Affairs and the Ministry of Defence have also led to drawbacks for the Assam Rifles, specifically. The Ministry of Home Affairs holds operational control over the Assam Rifles, while the Ministry of Defence supplies its officer cadres with Army officers. This has led to a lack of officers in the ranks of the Assam Rifles, affecting the organisation's performance and, to a large degree, the level of discipline of its troops[25].

The issue in Jammu & Kashmir has become the forefront issue for all administrations in New Delhi, in the field of its security agendas. This has resulted in all attention being directed to the valley, failing to give other issues such as the militancy in the Northeast its due importance. This resulted in a lack of inadequate manpower and deficit in resources directed to the region. In Kashmir, the Central Reserve Police Force is the prime CAPF on duty. It currently has 61 Battalions deployed in the Union Territory. In all of its theatres of operations, the CRPF, as well as other CAPF branches, have learned the value of being portrayed as a soft, peacemaker in the eyes of the local population, making the force more acceptable, approachable and trustable in ensuring an environment of peace, stability and progress. The operational potency of the CRPF is also linked to its sheer size, even after a reduction in the number of battalions following an improvement in the situation and implementation of New Delhi's confidence-building measures in the state. The force remains present in a majority of the militancy marred zone. Such uninterrupted deployment has ensured continuity in policy decisions and also their implementation[130].

Recommendations

For any security personnel in any theatre of operations, be it in the Red Belt, the Northeast or the Kashmir Valley; be it in close-quarter combat in the jungles or the valleys, or long-range scenarios along the borders of the Republic, the trooper's best friend will always be his/her service rifle. While the Central government decided to phase out the L1A1 Self Loading Rifles (SLR) and the obsolete Lee-Enfield bolt-action rifles from the Indian Army's inventory during the early 1990s, many of these scrapped weapons were handed over to CAPFs till the entry of the indigenously developed INSAS rifle in the late 1990s.

The INSAS is a gas-operated 5.56×45 mm assault rifle, capable of firing 600 RPM up to an effective range of 400 m. While the weapon won the war of 1999 in Kargil, there have been several complaints by its operators. Some issues include gun jamming, rifle going into automatic mode when it was set for three-round bursts and oil falling on the operators' eyes. Even during the 1999 war, soldiers of the Indian Army had complained of the rifle's ever often jamming and its cheap, plastic magazine cracking during combat operations at critically low temperatures[26] – a prominent climatic feature of the notorious region. With the CRPF itself having almost 300,000 active personnel, the central government approved the acquisition of an initial batch of 36,000 AK series rifles for quick import and induction into the force[27]. Around about 250,000 active BSF personnel guard the border with the rogue terror state that is Pakistan and the porous border with Bangladesh. This branch of the CAPF also relies upon the ageing and incompetent INSAS standard service rifle. Other CAPFs like the ITBP, CISF and SSB also suffer from modern infantry combat weapons platform shortage and are equipped with the INSAS. There is an urgent need to gradually begin processes of acquiring arms for all active duty CAPF troopers with cutting edge assault rifles.

An important move for the Ministry of Home Affairs would be to amend and adjust the mandates of each of the CAPFs:

- In the Northeast, the struggle between the Ministries of Home Affairs and Defence prevent the Assam Rifles suffers from having to play dual roles as both an internal security agency as well as a border guarding agency. Since the Assam Rifles have comfortable goodwill among the people of the region, their continuance as an internal security agency would be in the best interests of all (friendly) actors in the region. Handing over of border guarding responsibilities to other wings of the CAPF such as the BSF, SSB or ITBP, or the establishment of a new agency to handle the Indo-Myanmar border would relieve the Assam Rifles immensely, and improve the leadership's – which is already limited due to lack of officer's cadre – the ability to focus on counter-insurgency and peacekeeping roles.
- In the red belt of Central and East India, almost all branches of the CAPF, including border guard organisations, are present. While there already exists friction between state and central level inter-agency cooperation, the presence of multiple central agencies also poses the issue

of immense cooperation and logistical issues, both in the field of conduct of operations as well as gathering intelligence. The Central Reserve Police Force is the largest and most active participant in the war against left-wing extremism. The Ministry of Home Affairs must actively consider restricting central-government involvement in operations in the theatre to this agency.

- In Kashmir, the BSF was the CAPF of choice of New Delhi, until 2005. Being a border guard organisation, the BSF had had no prior experience or expertise in the field of counter-insurgency and terrorism. The CRPF, which was and remains the prime counter-insurgency force replaced the BSF eventually. It should therefore be of utmost importance to ensure that the Ministry of Home Affairs very clearly distinguishes the roles and mandates of its central armed police forces as per their areas of expertise and operational capabilities. Border guard organisations must guard the borders and internal security agencies must handle insurgency and militancy.

Another prospect for New Delhi to consider could be the unification of the several paramilitary forces of the Republic. Inter-departmental and inter-organisational conflict leads to nought but chaos and poses a major drawback in the field of cooperation, coordination and the synergising of efforts, that are meant to lead to the common goal of ensuring internal security and stability of the state. The Central Armed Police Forces, as mentioned before, can have their tasks divided into two major roles: as national border guarding forces (BSF, ITBP, SSB, AR), and as security, law & order, and counter-terror/insurgency forces (CISF, CRPF, NSG, AR). Based on these two distinct roles, the several paramilitary organisations under the helm of the Ministry of Home Affairs can be unified into two organisations, each handling the specifically assigned role. In such a case, the mandate of the two resulting organisations would be made very clear and would be more specialised, while at the same time preventing inter-organisational feud.

The Ministry must also look into the personal and character development of soldiers and officers in the ranks of the CAPF to ensure that the organisations do not face leadership crises, the way they are currently facing in the red belt and the Northeast. Along the same lines, the Government of India must promote the development of strategic thought and culture in the field of paramilitary forces and internal security, the same way it has through the establishment of military think-tanks, supporting civilian initiatives and entrance into the largely undiscussed field. Organisations such as CLAWS, NMF, CAPS, USI, IDSA et cetera only promote the further development and enhancement of knowledge in the respective fields of research. The creation of and ensuring the availability of knowledge and thought in this field will only support the CAPF, through the multiplication of the availability of knowledge, ensuring that the future generation of commandants and decision-makers of the Central Armed Police Forces are more capable and thorough in the choices they make; the choices that will ultimately have an impact on the future of the peace and stability of the country.

Notes

1. Ministry of Home Affairs, Government of India. (2017, October 8). Fatalities in Left-wing Extremism: 1999-2016* (MHA). Retrieved from South Asia Terrorism Portal: https://web.archive.org/web/20171008023622/http://www.satp.org/satporgtp/countries/india/maoist/data_sheets/fatalitiesnaxalmha.htm
2. WikiLeaks. (2013, September 9). Naxal Groups in India. Retrieved from WikiLeaks: https://wikileaks.org/gifiles/docs/64/64893_naxal-groups-in-india-.html
3. The Economic Times. (2015, August 4). Government signs landmark Nagaland peace treaty with NSCN(I-M) in presence of PM Narendra Modi. Retrieved from The Economic Times: https://economictimes.indiatimes.com/news/politics-and-nation/government-signs-landmark-nagaland-peace-treaty-with-nscni-m-in-presence-of-pm-narendra-modi/articleshow/48332059.cms
4. The Economic Times. (2015, August 4). Government signs landmark Nagaland peace treaty with NSCN(I-M) in presence of PM Narendra Modi. Retrieved from The Economic Times: https://economictimes.indiatimes.com/news/politics-and-nation/government-signs-landmark-nagaland-peace-treaty-with-nscni-m-in-presence-of-pm-narendra-modi/articleshow/48332059.cms
5. South Asia Terrorism Portal. (2017, December 24). Terrorist/Insurgent Groups - Manipur. Retrieved from South Asia Terrorism Portal: https://www.satp.org/satporgtp/countries/india/states/manipur/terrorist_outfits/index.html
6. South Asia Terrorism Portal. (2019, June 23). Fatalities in Terrorist Violence in India's Northeast 1992-2019. Retrieved from South Asia Terrorism Portal: https://www.satp.org/satporgtp/countries/india/database/fatalitiesnorteast2006.htm
7. South Asia Terrorism Portal. (n.d.). Terrorist/Extremist/Insurgent Groups - Jammu and Kashmir. Retrieved from South Asia Terrorism Portal: https://www.satp.org/satporgtp/countries/india/states/jandk/terrorist_outfits/terrorists_list_j&k.htm
8. South Asia Terrorism Portal. (2017). Fatalities in Jammu and Kashmir: 1990-2017. Retrieved from South Asia Terrorism Portal: https://www.satp.org/satporgtp/countries/india/states/jandk/data_sheets/Fatalities_mha.htm
9. Ministry of Home Affairs. (2018, April 30). About the Ministry. Retrieved from Ministry of Home Affairs: https://www.mha.gov.in/about-us/about-the-ministry
10. Central Reserve Police Force. (2020, July 27). About Us. Retrieved from Central Reserve Police Force: https://crpf.gov.in/about-us.htm
11. Central Industrial Security Force. (2020, November 2). Home. Retrieved from Central Industrial Security Force: https://www.cisf.gov.in/cisfeng/
12. Central Industrial Security Force. (2020, November 2). About CISF. Retrieved from Central Industrial Security Force: https://www.cisf.gov.in/cisfeng/about-us/
13. Border Security Force. (2020). Roles of the BSF. Retrieved from Border Security Force: https://bsf.gov.in/Role?LangId=dHJ1ZQ==

14. Indo-Tibetan Border Police. (2020, November 1). Origin of ITBP, the "HIMVEERS" and National Security. Retrieved from Indo-Tibetan Border Police: http://itbpolice.nic.in/itbpwebsite/Aboutus_new/history&role/history&role.html
15. Indo-Tibetan Border Police. (2020, November 1). Tasks of ITBP. Retrieved from Indo-Tibetan Border Police: http://itbpolice.nic.in/itbpwebsite/Aboutus_new/history&role/htmnav.html
16. Assam Rifles. (n.d.). History of Assam Rifles: 185 Years of Glory and Sacrifice. Retrieved from Assam Rifles: https://www.assamrifles.gov.in/english/newwindow.html?2030
17. Sashastra Seema Bal. (2020, October 6). Role of Sashastra Seema Bal. Retrieved from Sashastra Seema Bal: https://ssb.nic.in/index1.aspx?lsid=38&lev=2&lid=10&langid=1&Cid=0
18. Sashastra Seema Bal. (2020, October 6). Role of Sashastra Seema Bal. Retrieved from Sashastra Seema Bal: https://ssb.nic.in/index1.aspx?lsid=38&lev=2&lid=10&langid=1&Cid=0
19. Sashastra Seema Bal. (2020, October 6). Force Profile. Retrieved from Sashastra Seema Bal: https://ssb.nic.in/index1.aspx?lsid=37&lev=2&lid=9&langid=1&Cid=0
20. Press Information Bureau. (2019, January 8). Repeal of AFSPA. Retrieved from Press Information Bureau: https://pib.gov.in/Pressreleaseshare.aspx?PRID=1559119#:~:text=Presently%2C%20AFSPA%2C%201958%20is%20operational,of%20Arunachal%20Pradesh%2C%20bordering%20the
21. Unofficial name; not used by MHA or GoI
22. Routray, B. P. (2013). India's internal wars: counterinsurgency role of central police forces. Small Wars & Insurgencies, 24(4), 648-668.
23. Gupta, S. (2010, April 23). Dantewada massacre: Probe finds command failure. Retrieved from The Indian Express: https://indianexpress.com/article/news-archive/web/dantewada-massacre-probe-finds-command-failure/
24. Routray, B. P. (2013). India's internal wars: counterinsurgency role of central police forces. Small Wars & Insurgencies, 24(4), 648-668.
25. Routray, B. P. (2013). India's internal wars: counterinsurgency role of central police forces. Small Wars & Insurgencies, 24(4), 648-668.
26. Singh, S. (2019, March 4). How AK-203, superior to INSAS, will end forces' hunt for a reliable rifle. Retrieved from The Times of India: https://timesofindia.indiatimes.com/india/how-ak-203-superior-to-insas-will-end-forces-hunt-for-a-reliable-rifle/articleshow/68248283.cms
27. Geopolitics. (2020, August). Modernising the Paramilitary. Retrieved from Magzter: https://www.magzter.com/article/Military-Defence/Geopolitics/MODERNISING-THE-PARAMILITARY

7

Integrated Information Networks

The digital age poses new security threats but also provides opportunities to make India's defence architecture ever more effective and efficient by allowing for seamless, real time situational awareness. This is particularly important given that many of India's competitors are adept at centrally accumulating and operationalizing information from all branches of their armed forces. Relative to this, India is yet to establish such capabilities limited by slow technological improvement, budget restrictions, and fewer deeper strategic collaborations. Thus, the importance of integrating information within and between the three defence services, and between intelligence agencies is paramount. It is also a crucial pillar towards India's efforts to solidify its network centric warfare capabilities that requires coordinated collection and sharing of information and ensuring that all elements of India's security architecture are set towards this direction. The first steps towards that goal have been taken with the creation of a centralized chain of command for the three services through the post of the Chief of Defence Staff. However, much more needs to be done subsequently at lower levels (such as the level of individual ministries and the three services) for this macro level change to be truly effective.

As of today, India possesses some level of information systems integration at the level of each service and has plans for an Integrated Defence Communication Network. It also possesses information collection and sharing infrastructure in collaboration with regional and international allies along with integrated information collection infrastructure for counter-terrorism efforts. At the level of each service the following capabilities exist: The Indian army currently uses an "Operational Information System" (OIS) and a "Management Information System" (MIS). Initial work on a Battlefield Management System (BMS) began in 2011, but progress was stalled in 2017 after the program was halted. The Air Force uses the "Air Force Network" or AFNet and the "Integrated Air Command and Control System" (IACCS) for information sharing. Finally, the Indian Navy operates the Naval Communications Network and the Naval Combat Management System (CMS) in some vessels. India also operates the National Intelligence Grid (NATGRID) that integrates data from various avenues and makes it available to different government agencies such as the CBI, NIA, R&AW, and the IB.

Military Networks

Indian Army

Some of these aforementioned networks are already quite outdated and are in urgent need of digitization. One means of doing so is through the digitization of databases through the use of secure cloud services that allow for seamless information sharing. In the case of the Army's OIS and MIS, the first steps towards this were taken in 2015 through the creation of the Army's personal cloud database for "operational and personnel information such as deployments, movements of formations, and health and service records"[1] in collaboration between the Department of Telecommunications and the Ministry of Defence. In 2019 this was followed up with efforts to expand the army's cloud capacity that would provide for greater bandwidth capabilities. This would allow the army to store footage, digitize ground formations, boost software and hardware updates to the existing infrastructure[2].

Indian Navy

The Navy is quickly catching up with a multiyear contract with Sterlite Tech for a Naval Communications Network (NCN). The NCN was inaugurated in 2019 at the INS Valsura, Jamnagar and will likely see many additions and upgrades given the navy's contract with Sterlite to "design, build, and manage" the network over the next decade[3]. The project's goal is to connect multiple naval facilities to each other, including those in Indian administered islands, to facilitate efficient information sharing, install secure data centres, allow for new applications on the network that enhance real-time situational awareness, data analytics, and more[4]. Currently the navy also operates an AI powered Naval Combat Management System aboard the INS Vikrant. While this CMS has been applied only to the INS Vikrant, the defence agencies have been investigating the feasibility of integrated AI systems into indigenous integrated information networks and this move marks a step in the right direction towards that goal.

Indian Air Force

Finally, the Indian Air Force operates the "Air Force Network" or "AFNet". AFNet was first established in 2010 in an effort to bring the Air Force on par with connectivity standards required by India's goal of Network Centric Operations.

The information network is meant to allow for "video from Unmanned Aerial Vehicle (UAV), pictures from an AWACS aircraft to the decision-makers on ground sitting hundreds of kilometres away, providing intelligence inputs from far-flung areas at central locations seamlessly"[5]. AFNet also allows for the Integrated Air Command and Control System, that integrates the service's ground based and airborne sensors and systems into the network. However, with the rapid pace of technological change and the end of AFNet's purported lifecycle in 2017, the system is at risk of becoming outdated. A second-generation iteration of AFNet has been in the works but was postponed in 2017 until 2020. Given that the 2020 Coronavirus Pandemic has put a significant damper on the defence sector as a whole it is possible that AFNet 2.0 will take longer than desirable to materialize.

Tri-Forces Information Network Integration

Given the network capabilities that exist within each service, the logical next step is to establish information integration across all three services. The Armed Forces joint doctrine stated that "survivable secure and alternate means of communication for smooth flow of data and information, effective networking and inter-Service integration, automation and inter-operability is quintessential today"[6]. Thus, the creation of the tri-forces wide Integrated Defence Communication Network (DCN), actualized in 2016, is a significant step forward which allows the forces improved situational awareness and decision-making capacity. The plan is also an important element in larger efforts to help centralize and streamline India's military command. A statement by HCL Infosystems, the system's manufacturer, reiterated this fact by stating that the "DCN is a major step towards ensuring network centricity across the three services, the Integrated Defence Staff (IDS) headquarters and the Strategic Forces Command (SFC)"[7].

Satellite Surveillance

Another important element of information network are the space based satellites that are instrumental in collecting and rapidly transmitting information to the services. The GSAT-7 has been indispensable to the Indian Navy in providing and relaying real time intelligence on ship movements and networking with 60 ships and 75 aircrafts during exercises in 2014 and has effectively expanded India's surveillance capacity up to the Strait of Malacca[8]. The satellite's success prompted the launch of the GSAT-7a for joint use by the Indian Air Force and the Indian Army as well as plans for a new upgraded GSAT-7r for the Indian Navy. These satellites are a crucial piece of the puzzle by generating information in real time. It serves as a reminder that a viable integrated information network must have the capacity to efficiently source relevant data in addition to collating and processing it. In this sense the launch of the GSAT series has set India on a path of success.

International Collaborations

SAGAR Related Information Integration Efforts

SAGAR - Security and Growth for All in the Region - is a relatively newer concept originating in a 2015 Speech by Prime Minister Modi that outlines the country's plans for the Indian Ocean Region. Under the banner of SAGAR cooperation has been secured or is being built in six key elements: Security, Capacity Building, Collective Action, sustainability, Maritime Engagement, Regional Connectivity. SAGAR works on these multiple fronts to secure India's security, diplomatic and environmental interest in the IOR in tandem with its regional partners with a key focus on cooperation and collective action. This emphasis on cooperation and collective action has allowed SAGAR to become a platform for the creation of agencies that serve to collect, analyse, and disseminate information on issues of maritime security, environmental concerns, etc. Two primary security centric networks created are the Information Fusion Centre - Indian Ocean region and coastal surveillance Radar System.

Information Fusion Centre - Indian Ocean Region

The Information Fusion Centre headquartered in Gurugram marks India's latest attempt at boosting its security in the Indian Ocean Region (IOR) given the prevalence of piracy, maritime terrorist, illegal fishing and poaching, trafficking, etc[9]. The centre is aimed at coordinating with resource centres across the region to enhance situation awareness by "undertaking collation, fusion and dissemination of this data being exchanged with all partners"[10]. Currently the fusion centre liaisons with several major information centre: Virtual Regional Maritime Traffic Centre (VRMTC), Maritime Security Centre - Horn of Africa (MSCHOA), Regional Cooperation Agreement on Combating Piracy and Armed Robbery (ReCAAP), Information Fusion Centre-Singapore (IFC-SG), and International Maritime Bureau - Piracy Reporting Centre (IMB PRC)[11]. The centre is also in the process of setting up liaison offices for partner countries which have signed white shipping information exchange agreements with India[12].

Coastal Surveillance Radar System

The efforts towards a coastal radar network began after the 26/11 attacks to ensure increased maritime domain awareness. While the network began with the installation of radars across the Indian coastline the operation has since been scaled up significantly and now encompasses domestic and foreign actors. The Indian coast guard operates a network of radars, electro optics, very high frequency radio communications and meteorological units across mainland India and Indian territories that can track vessels on sea. This network is also being extended further in a second phase of the project. Most recently in 2020 state run Bharat Electronics Limited started work on 38 new radars along the Indian coast to fill existing gaps[13]. Since its inception the network has expanded to include neighbouring allies such as Maldives, Sri Lanka, Seychelles, and Mauritius. A set of 10 radar were under construction, three of which are being upgraded, in the Maldives in 2019 making them the most recent addition to the Coastal Radar Chain[14]. The Coastal Surveillance Radar System combined with the new Information Fusion Centre will prove to be a productive force in enhancing maritime domain awareness of the Indian navy.

Indo-Pacific Oceans Initiative

The Indo-Pacific Oceans Initiative was first introduced in the 2019 East Asia Summit as an effort to create a cohesive mechanism for cooperation between India and its ASEAN partners. The IPOI works on issues of Maritime Security; Maritime Ecology; Maritime Resources; Capacity Building and Resource Sharing; Disaster Risk Reduction and Management; Science, Technology and Academic Cooperation; and Trade Connectivity and Maritime Transport[15]. The aim is to further integrate ASEAN and India in their effort's todays greater maritime security and awareness. The ASEAN-India Plan of Action states the importance of further information sharing and collection mechanisms and states that these, in addition to other security related objectives, will be considered in light of India's IPOI initiative[16]. While little has been done under the banner of IPOI as of yet, it can be a powerful driver for progress in the region with the help of ASEAN integration. This will likely involve the creation of newer mechanisms for information collection and the use of existing ones such as the Information Fusion Centre-IOR.

Intelligence Networks

NATGRID

The National Intelligence Grid (NATGRID) was first envisioned in 2008 as a one stop shop for all domestic intelligence agencies to aid their counter-terror efforts. The network complies data from 21 sectors such as banking, immigration, police, telecom, tax record etc., and makes them available to 11 agencies, namely the: Research and Analysis Wing (R&AW), National Investigation Agency (NIA), Intelligence Bureau (IB), Central Bureau of Investigation (CBI), Financial Intelligence Unit (FIU), Central Board of Direct Taxes (CBDT), Directorate of Revenue Intelligence (DRI), Enforcement Directorate (ED), Narcotics Control Bureau (NCB), Central Board of Indirect Taxes and Customs (CBIC) and Directorate General of GST Intelligence[17]. The grid runs on an algorithm that allows for big data analysis and to "generate trends and leads for organization to follow up"[18]. Officials ensure that the system will remain highly secure and leave an auditable trail of its use. The grid is set to be functional by December 2020; however, it has not yet materialized.

Recommendations

More research and development into the viability of AI in defence operations must be conducted. The advantages of AI integrated information networks are countless, including providing faster and smarter data analysis. The use of AI operated systems is already under way through the 2018 government-initiated AI Task Force which outlined Lethal Autonomous Weapon Systems (LAWS), unmanned surveillance, simulated war games and training, cyber-security, aerospace security, and intelligence & reconnaissance[19]. In addition to these an AI operated battlefield management system is already functional in the Indian aircraft carrier INS Vikramaditya. Integrated information networks can provide a plethora of present and past data that can be instrumental in allowing for machine learning that would aid AI in better formulating future projections of the strategic environment and appropriate strategies to aid human decision making. The use of AI deserves further consideration as the more integrated information agencies look to not only centrally collecting data but also operationalizing it in ever more nuanced and multidimensional ways. For instance, the data that the Information Fusion Centre collects to increase domain awareness is analysed to provide "detection and prediction of emergent threats" in the region[20]. AI might help boost such functions.

Integrating AI functions in existing or new systems will be a painstaking but important task. Other than the task of training AI systems, India must formulate a clear tri-service wide AI strategy that outlines their vision of what AI can provide for the armed services and how AI might be integrated into the various systems, new and old alike. It is also important to note that Artificial Intelligence is still an emerging field with much to discover through research and development. It is important to acknowledge that there are gaps between the organizations where the needs assessment relating to such technologies takes place, government agencies, and the organizations that are at the cutting edge of developing AI, universities and private companies.

It is crucial that these gaps are filled in through collaboration between universities and the MOD. Such a plan of action was adopted by the United States military for its own military AI research[21]. Finally, it is important to note that while much work remains on developing the technical capacity for integrating AI into the security apparatus, even more work remains in crafting regulation to ensure that such technologies are used responsibly. Much has been written and shown in literature and pop-culture about the dangers of AI. While not always factually accurate, AI, if left unregulated, can pose technical and ethical dilemmas later on. For instance, an AI's performance is only as good as the data that is inputted. Thus, an AI's solutions may not always be fool proof and the AI might "fail in unintended or unanticipated ways"[22]. There may also be issues over trust in systems. In such a case, it would also be necessary for India to describe what the relationship between AI and people would be as AI continued to be integrated into more systems. Thus, regulatory frameworks must not be left behind technical capabilities if India wishes to remain ahead of the curve and ensure that technology is used responsibly.

As India expands its network capabilities it must ensure that this is done at several levels. Currently efforts towards digitization and information integration have involved establishing data centres and nodal agencies. However, integration must be accomplished right from the level of agency to the level of the individual. Currently the Indian armed forces use the now archaic tactical communications system that was set to be revamped in 2000. Yet efforts to do so have only begun in mid 2010s as news of private sector companies engaging with the government on the subject appeared relatively more consistently. Till date there has not been any report of a new Tactical Communications network being inaugurated that would replace the old one in its entirety.

Seamless communication can help greatly in the transfer of information about the battlefield, in terms of images, videos, etc., in real time. Yet it seems that the administration is currently not devoting sufficient resources to this sector. There is constant rhetoric around the need for military modernization in and around the defence sector, yet it is important to note that efforts towards modernization must reach even the most peripheral seeming elements that are essential to ensuring that information integration occurs reliably. The lack of modern communications networks in the army and slow procurement of the same in the navy and the air force is one such element that may slow progress towards the modernization of the Indian military's communications network. Thus, the focus must be to provide greater investment to ensure that these information systems are up and running faster. It is also important to ensure that there is capacity for tactical data linking between the communication's networks of the three forces. This should be a task that the new integrated defence staff can appropriate to a new or existing agency under it.

Regardless of extensive development of information networks and cloud capacities, the prospects of integrated information networks will only be as efficient as the bandwidth they function on allows them to be. Thus, the importance of 4G, 5G, and even 6G technology that facilitate the military's bandwidth needs, or may do so in the future, cannot be underestimated. India currently operates on a 4G network that allows for data transfer speeds of around 1 Gigabytes per second. While numbers vary a 5G network could provide speeds that are 10 to 100 times faster than a 4G network. A 5G network also boasts lower latencies and allows for much higher density of devices to function at one go. Most countries in the world are struggling to 5G enable their defence networks due to lack of access to the necessary technologies and India is no exception. India currently lacks the capacity to research and develop its own 5G technology and cannot reliably gain such capabilities from Huawei, the largest provider of 5G infrastructure, either given the risks to security that may pose.

Thus, India can only rely on other 5G providers and/or develop 5G capabilities indigenously. The safest bet, from a security perspective, would be to develop capacity domestically. While the Indian government has launched its own initiative to test newly developed 5G systems, greater collaboration with the private sector would also be fruitful. The Indian private sector, through companies like Jio, are ahead of the curve in terms of developing a 5G solution. The Ministry of Defence and the Ministry of Technology should also work to develop a nexus of government actors, private sector actors, research universities, etc., to encourage closer collaboration and spur the development of domestic solution to the 5G issue. Development of future infrastructure that is 5G and 6G compatible will allow agencies more room to play around with these technologies and design better strategies.

Notes

1. Gurung, S.K. (2019, June 04). Army plans cloud storage for operations data. Retrieved from The Economic Times: https://economictimes.indiatimes.com/news/defence/army-plans-cloud-storage-for-operations-data/articleshow/69643144.cms?from=mdr
2. Ibid.
3. Sterlite Tech. (2018, February 26). Sterlite Tech to Build Next Gen Communications Network for the Indian Navy. Retrieved from Sterlite Tech: https://www.stl.tech/press_release/601.html
4. Abbas, M. (2018, October 16). Indian Navy ropes in Sterlite Tech to deploy secure digital network. Retrieved from Economic Times: https://economictimes.indiatimes.com/news/defence/indian-navy-ropes-in-sterlite-tech-to-deploy-secure-digital-network/articleshow/66234464.cms?from=mdr

5. Indian Airforce. (2010, September 14). ANTONY DEDICATES AFNET TO THE NATION. Retrieved from Indian Air Force Press Release: https://web.archive.org/web/20100922122516/http://indianairforce.nic.in/show_pressrelease.php?pg_id=107&news_id=562
6. Integrated Defence Staff. (2017, April). Joint Doctrine Indian Armed Forces. Retrieved from: https://bharatshakti.in/wp-content/uploads/2015/09/Joint_Doctrine_Indian_Armed_Forces.pdf
7. IANS. (2016, June 30). Indian armed forces get converged communication network. Retrieved from The Hindustan Times: https://www.hindustantimes.com/india-news/indian-armed-forces-get-converged-communication-network/story-qVvbLYosFAdhT2l0mLSVwI.html
8. Gupta, J. (2014, March 11). Indian Navy joins search for missing Malaysian plane in the Malacca Straits. Retrieved from The Times of India: https://timesofindia.indiatimes.com/india/Indian-Navy-joins-search-for-missing-Malaysian-plane-in-the-Malacca-Straits/articleshow/31855418.cms
9. Information Fusion Center. Information Fusion Center – India Ocean Region. About Us. Retrieved from https://www.indiannavy.nic.in/ifc-ior/about-us.html.
10. Ibid.
11. Peri, D. (2019, October 07). India starts sharing maritime data. Retrieved from The Hindu: https://www.thehindu.com/news/national/india-starts-sharing-maritime-data/article29611936.ece
12. Peri, D. (2019, October 07). India starts sharing maritime data. Retrieved from The Hindu: https://www.thehindu.com/news/national/india-starts-sharing-maritime-data/article29611936.ece
13. IANS. (2020, February 10). BEL to enhance Indian coastal surveillance system. Retrieved from Outlook India: https://www.outlookindia.com/newsscroll/bel-to-enhance-indian-coastal-surveillance-system/1730386
14. Pubby, M. (2019, April 23). Work resumes full stream on Maldives coastal radar. Retrieved from The Economic Times: https://economictimes.indiatimes.com/news/defence/work-resumes-full-steam-on-maldives-coastal-radars/articleshow/69000819.cms?from=mdr
15. Ministry of External Affairs. (2020, February 07). Indo-Pacific Division Briefs. Retrieved from the Ministry of External Affairs: https://mea.gov.in/Portal/ForeignRelation/Indo_Feb_07_2020.pdf
16. ASEAN. (2020, September 12). PLAN OF ACTION TO IMPLEMENT THE ASEAN-INDIA PARTNERHSIP FOR PEACE, PROGRESS AND SHARED PROSPERITY (2021-2025). Retrieved from ASEAN: https://asean.org/storage/2020/09/ASEAN-India-POA-2021-2025-Final.pdf
17. Press Trust of India. (2019, September 22). National intelligence Grid to be ready by early 2020. Retrieved from India Today: https://www.indiatoday.in/india/story/national-intelligence-grid-to-be-ready-by-early-2020-1601949-2019-09-22
18. Sen, S.R. (2020, January 30). NATGRID, India's tech powered database to fight terror, to roll out in the March. Retrieved from Hindustan Times: https://www.hindustantimes.com/india-news/govt-to-roll-out-database-for-real-time-info-on-terror-soon/story-rXSmbGMGQVRzosGdc7JdhM.html
19. The Artificial Intelligence Task Force. (2018, March 20). Report of The Artificial Intelligence Task Force. Retrieved from Department for Industrial Policy & Promotion:

https://dipp.gov.in/sites/default/files/Report_of_Task_Force_on_ArtificialIntelligence_20March2018_2.pdf

20. Sarangi, S. (2019). Unpacking SAGAR (Security and Growth for All in the Region). Retrieved from United Service Institution of India: https://usiofindia.org/wp-content/uploads/2020/02/USI-Occasional-Paper_2_19-Unpacking-SAGAR-Final-print-File-1.pdf
21. Federal Laboratory Consortium. (2020, November 23). Army, DoD team with Howard University on AI center of excellence. Retrieved from Federal Laboratory Consortium: https://federallabs.org/news/army-dod-team-with-howard-university-on-ai-center-of-excellence
22. Morgan, F.E., et. All. (2020). Military Applications of Artificial Intelligence – Ethical Concerns in an Uncertain World. Retrieved from Rand Corporation: https://www.rand.org/pubs/research_reports/RR3139-1.html

8

Space and Cyber Security

Cyber and Space Security present new frontiers for Indian security. Rapid modernization has facilitated technological development like never before and this has created both opportunities and challenges. India must be in a position to protect its people from the downsides of technological developments, while leveraging those very developments for its own strategic needs. Thus, there is an urgent need to take account of India's current cyber and space security capabilities and where there is scope for improvement.

Cyber Security

Reliance on digital tools is at an all- time high and digitization of information is increasingly becoming the standard method of operation in defence sectors. Yet the digital scape comes with its own challenges and vulnerabilities. With time, both the frequency and intensity of cyber-attacks gets more frequent and complex in India[1]. Such attacks come in all shapes and sizes, including phishing, ransomware, data theft, malware, Dos attacks, and more. The most prominent targets are financial, healthcare, and public sector infrastructure but defence entities are also at immense risk of being compromised. There is growing reliance on cloud-based services for data storage, internet reliant communication for aircrafts, ships, weapons, and ground-based equipment which has created an "internet of military things" that is now vulnerable to both independent and government hackers. One report has found that India's nuclear installation are also at significant risk of becoming victims of cyber warfare[2]. In context of these challenges India's efforts to counter cyber warfare are quite limited and a fuller investigation of current capabilities and future possibilities is necessary.

India's Cyber Security Frameworks and Institutions

India realizes that cybersecurity poses a serious threat to security of its military and civilian assets. In an effort to respond to such a crisis there has been steady effort to create the institutional and doctrinal frameworks around what India's cyber security and cyber warfare goals and requirements are. The most recent and substantial of these efforts have been the creation of the CERT, with their most recent report charting India's security challenges in 2013, the 2013 National Cyber Security Policy, The National Technical Research Organization, and the proposed national 'Defence Cyber Agency'. The National Cyber Security Framework in particular lays out a range of strategies some of which have indeed seen implementation. For example, the report recommends the creation of a national nodal agency as part of larger efforts to create a "secure cyber ecosystem" which has partially translated into the Defence Cyber Agency[3].

Other than the CERT and the National Cyber Security Strategy there are multiple organization level strategies for dealing with cyber security. Yet, in terms of the civilian sectors most of the government provided efforts focused on dealing with security issues faced by state-run agencies, banks, and other infrastructure creating a lapse in coverage. Despite their immense contribution, bodies like CERT also tend to coordinate between various organizations rather than integrate them to create one unified response to threats of cyber security. While there is no one organization serving this goal in terms of integrated response for both defence and civilian sectors, the Defence Cyber Agency is to take on this role for the Army, Navy, and Air Force. The response to cyber security issues has also been largely reactive and not proactive considering that technology is growing at ever higher rates which are not matched by the pace of new regulation and strategy. The fact that after the 2013 National Cyber Security Strategy there has not been another national security strategy despite assurances of one being available by the start of 2020 is an indicator of this.

Current Capabilities for Cyber Security and Cyber Warfare in the Military

Currently all three branches of the armed forces are working towards the goal of network centric warfare. Network centric warfare holds seamless flow of information as one of its key pillars which in turn requires greater connectivity, which is often internet enabled, between people and equipment. The Joint Doctrine of The Armed Forces reinforces this fact by stating that "a comprehensive cyber force structure drives capabilities in cyber war fighting and wins network centric wars"[4]. Additionally, there is growing interest in developing capacity for cyber warfare and incorporating Artificial Intelligence into warfare. India also faces unprecedented levels of cyber-attacks every day. Indeed a 2017 study found that India is ranked third in number of cyber-attacks experienced; while many of them happen to civilian sources, military installations are not spared. In 2019 the Army dealt with 23 cyber-attacks averaging out to almost two attacks every month[5]. Given these realities it is increasingly important that the massive quantities of sensitive security data that is produced regularly is secured. This is why cyber security is crucial to the armed forces.

A central challenge for India's endeavours in cyber security and cyber warfare is that it approaches the issue from an overwhelmingly defensive posture. The current focus is less on detecting or preventing attacks ahead of time and more on dealing with attacks when they come. The 2013 National Cyber Security Strategy outlines several recommended strategies to improve India's response to cyber-attacks but doesn't delve into developing offensive capabilities. While this is not a negative focus in and of itself, taking a more defensive posture in the long term will put India on unstable footing internationally and compromise security domestically as well. A look at India's immediate neighbourhood quickly reveals the challenges that lack of offensive cyber warfare abilities can create. China and Pakistan have both mastered and instrumentalized cyberspace not only for spreading misinformation but also for allegedly launching attacks on systems within India[6]. Indeed, the PLA has been incredibly proactive in adopting cyber warfare tactics as of late with reports that there has been an uptick in alleged Chinese malware that were intended to steal sensitive intelligence. Given India's limited cyber warfare capabilities it will find it hard to reciprocate equally.

In building up offensive capabilities and bolstering existing infrastructure there are certain existing hurdles to overcome. Firstly, much of the equipment used towards cyber security is not indigenously developed. Instead, India relies on internationally sourced parts, such as chips, processors, software, etc., for developing and maintaining its cyber security infrastructure. This means that system can potentially be vulnerable to new backdoors to the system. Current efforts, like the creation of indigenous cloud systems in collaboration with Indian tech companies, must be reinforced by wider efforts for indigenous production of other hardware and software as well.

Currently there are several organizations that strategize and implement cyber security measures individually and many others that can contribute to enhancing cyber warfare capabilities. The way cyberwarfare is thought of within military institutions in particular is narrow relative to international contemporaries. For example, the 2018 Indian Army Land Warfare Doctrine finds that cyber warfare and electronic warfare are two distinct functions under the umbrella of information warfare[7]; yet, China has long understood that the two are much more lethal when used in conjunction[8]. This represents not only a gap in ability but also a gap in outlook. India must develop a stronger framework that approaches issues of cyber security and warfare in more potent and novel ways. If this is not done in earnest India will only ever be a reactive cyber force. India must develop Cyber warfare capabilities to cover existing gaps so as to meet existing challenges it faces and aim to exceed China if it wishes to gain advantage over them in the domain of cyber warfare.

Looking into the reason for the limits in capacity leads us to consider another dilemma facing India concerning the development of its cyber capabilities. One reason for India's limited offensive capabilities, as was exemplified in the paragraph above, is limited interactions between relevant departments that could help generate new conversations and solutions about what is attainable for India in cyberspace[9]. Adequate interaction between Indian Army Training Command (ARTRAC) and technical entities such as the Defence Intelligence Agency (DIA), the Corps of Signals, the Defence Information Assurance and Research Agency (DIARA), and the National Technical Reconnaissance Organisation (NTRO) could have provided military officials direction on how cyber warfare and electronic warfare capabilities could be leveraged towards land warfare[10]. While such an example highlights the need for broadening the scope of agencies consulted and brought within the loop, it also risks the creation of further smaller issue centric organizations that only add to the plethora of organizations working on various aspects of cyber security in various services. This adds to the urgency for a central organization, like the Defence Cyber agency, within the armed forces that can focus these efforts and harmonize them giving India's overall cyber security efforts a clear direction.

Recommendations

Currently the institutional infrastructure around cyber security is extensive but fragmented. Several key government departments are ornamented with their own cyber security divisions, the National Critical Information Infrastructure Protection Centre (NCIIPN) is the nodal agency for the country's information systems, the Data Security Council of India is a body overseeing data protection measures, the National Informatics Centre provides data storage and website maintenance for the government's internet presence. The newly created Defence Cyber Agency is another addition to this list. However, unlike the other agencies just mentioned, the Defence Cyber Agency aims at integrating the cyber security and cyber warfare operations of the three forces in addition to touching base with the operations of other agencies. This attempt at greater centralization should lead to a better system to organize the various nodal agencies and groups working on cyber security and cyber warfare so as to best connect necessary bodies and optimize their use. New collaborations between organizations and agencies must also be envisioned while ensuring that there exists a broad vision to work towards.

To this end the new defence cyber organization's most urgent task would be to outline a comprehensive and forward looking national cyber security and cyber warfare strategy and publish India's cyber security doctrine. Such a doctrine should elaborate on existing capacities, provide a comprehensive outline of agencies and departments engaged in cyber security operations and their collaborations, list any projects or policy measures in the pipeline, and elaborate on existing gaps in India's cyber security in terms of doctrine and practice. Finally, and perhaps most crucially, India must also outline the country's understanding of cyber security and how it wishes to integrate cyber security with other emerging fields such as information warfare, electronic warfare, and psychological war. Cyberwarfare in particular is a crucial element of informational warfare, an area where India is yet to match China's capacities.

Of course, work on a national cyber security and cyber warfare doctrine and renewed efforts towards strengthening and establishing new capacities requires substantial financial backing. Funding constraints, however, remain a consistent problem throughout the armed forces and finance for cyber security and warfare initiatives are no exception. One solution to this can be the development of indigenous technologies through adequate investment in research and development. This may require more investment into R&D in the short term, through the DRDO and the Ministry of Communication and Information Technology. Given India's past record of indigenous development producing relatively lower cost final products successfully, if provided with reliable flow of funding and the absence of ad hoc development, the investment will likely be worth the initial costs. This has the dual benefit of developing cost-effective alternatives and reducing reliance on foreign suppliers for sourcing parts. None the less, this shouldn't discount the value of seeking superior parts, system, software, etc., as it helps source quality resource presently and creates another avenue to connect governments and industries. The point remains that this cannot be the primary or the only solution.

Towards indigenization, India has taken significant steps towards this through the development of new data centres and establishing partnerships with the private sectors companies and government run corporations. As one report states there is no public and private in cyber security, all assets are equally at risk[11]. Thus, transparent private sector collaboration that is not bogged down by red-tape will allow for greater innovation and could help reduce some of the government's own R&D costs as well. One way to approach this would be to set up a panel or task force comprising of personnel from academia, businesses, and the government. The panel can tackle the task of creating a holistic foundation for public-private cooperation in the future by identifying where R&D is most urgently needed. It can also identify key areas in India's cyber security and cyber warfare infrastructure and policy that can benefit from upgrades and/or reform. Thus, such efforts should be started at earliest and should also be multiplied going forward.

Space Security

In the 2017 joint doctrine opening up of outer space as a new domain for exploration and use was described as a "revolution in military affairs"[12]. Indeed space, as the popular saying goes, is the final frontier and one that India has begun to conquer. While space has been used for civilian space programs, military use of space is a relatively newer phenomenon, particularly for India. Considerable strides have been made in terms of indigenous development of technology yet much more work remains. India lacks a clear and detailed game plan for India's military space strategy where its contemporaries such as the US, China, and Russia, are much farther into their efforts to weaponize space. To keep pace with the changing nature of modern "hybrid" warfare, there is an urgent need to build India's capacity as a space force in addition to goals of military modernization or cyber warfare.

The militarization of space has gradually occurred over the decades through the testing and launch of satellites dedicated for military use, counterspace weapons such as kinetic weapons which use warheads as their tool of choice and non-kinetic weapons such as lasers, EMP weapons, or high-powered microwave weapons. As the US and China particularly ramp up efforts to test new weaponry and launch new satellites, India, at its current capacity, is playing catch up. Data shows that while the number of space launches has increased significantly in the past 10 years, the rate is increasing much faster for China[13]. In addition to satellites, China is also ahead in terms of testing space weaponry. Thus, in order to gain a lead in space warfare India must increase technical capabilities, financial investment, and introduce doctrinal clarity in its vision for India's presence in space.

Current Capabilities

After China's 2007 ASAT weapons test India found its space assets vulnerable, triggering the need for an accelerated space defence program. Today the 2017 joint doctrine acknowledges space as a critical force multiplier for the armed forces, conveying India's desire to increase the use of space assets to assist military operations[14]. To this end, India is developing a range of kinetic and non-kinetic weapons to be used in space. India currently operates a range of launch vehicles, satellites, and missiles along with one dedicated launchpad operated by the Indian Space Research Organization (ISRO) and the Ministry of Defence . This partnership has shown incredible effectiveness and is a pillar of India's space defence goals. Currently the government relies on one polar satellite launch vehicle (PSLV) and one geosynchronous launch vehicle (GSLV) which are launched from the Satish Dhawan Space Centre, the country's only major space port. In 2017 ISRO accomplished the launch of 104 individual satellites from one PVSL, an international record, and the GSLV has been in use for launch of the GSAT series of satellites. ISRO also plans to use the GSLV for its first manned mission into space "Gaganyaan".

The last few years have seen particularly rapid developments in new counterspace arms and strategies. The most prominent of these has been the testing of India's first indigenous ASAT weapon in 2019 that added the country to the exclusive list of international powers that possess the ability to do so. Beyond this, counter space weapons are largely in the conceptualization and development phase. The 2019 ASAT weapon is a "direct ascent" variant and the government is undertaking R&D for a co-orbital ASAT weapon and non-kinetic weapons as well[15]. Non-Kinetic weapons provide significant benefits to any space force given that they are not regulated by international treaties and do not generate debris. At the current pace of development, it is unlikely that India will develop non-kinetic weapons in the coming years. Yet it is important to note that any holistic Indian space force that wishes to balance against regional rivals will be incomplete without one.

In addition to the given technical capabilities organization structure and strategy are equally critical for streamlining space operations. In 2010 the integrated space cell was initiated under the offices of the Integrated Defence Staff and was followed up by the Defence Space Agency (DSA) in 2019. The DSA will serve as a nodal agency that strategizes and coordinates between the IDS, the three services, and technical organization to chalk out the direction India will take in terms of military presence in space. The Integrated space cell and later the DSA were instrumental in facilitating the launch of GSAT satellites for the Navy, Amy, and Airforce and the ASAT. the IDS, soon after the creation of the DSA, has also helped coordinate a simulated space wargame which accounted for space powers like China, the US, and Russia, to gauge the threat of a space war and how India ought to respond. The simulation reinforced that "future wars may be dominated by activities in the cyber and space domains, leading to asymmetric advantages or disadvantages"[16]. Lastly, the Defence Space Research Agency will constitute another key piece of the puzzle providing specialized research and development into space usable weapons systems and technologies[17]. The organization will function under the DSA and the IDS. The current set-up is well on its way to solidify the centrality of space within India's defence strategy.

Public-Private Partnerships

India's endeavours in space are newer relative to its contemporaries and have relied considerably on the state's initiative to produce end results. While companies like SpaceX have sped past other private sector actors to manufacture and launch its own fleet of space crafts, India's private sector is nowhere near these levels of capacity. However, a more active private sector and more meaningful avenues for public-private collaboration must be explored to enable greater innovation and reduce the burden on ISRO. While ISRO officials has stated that the organization is not spreading itself too thin given its extensive to-do list, this may not always remain the case. In addition to the benefits a commercial space industry can provide India domestically, it can also allow India to interact with the international market for space technology further as well.

Currently India operates one fully owned company, the Antrix Corporation, that works as an arm of ISRO by managing its commercial activities. Antrix is charged with providing its customers with satellite systems and subsystems. It has its own facilities and a dedicated core of scientists and engineers that work on specialized designs for orders that come from clients abroad and at home. Yet, Antrix has been criticised for being to slow and inflexible in the current climate creating the need for a broader private sector strategy for space related technologies[18]. Today, the Indian space sector accounts for a mere 3% of the international space market and private companies are largely limited to the same component and satellite manufacturing roles that Antrix carries out[19]. It seems that the Indian government has moved to invite private companies into ISRO projects, perhaps having similarly realized the untapped potential of the private sector. The recently approved IN-SPACE, Indian National Space Promotion and Authorization Centre, will serve to augment current capacities in private companies and allow them access to ISRO resources to encourage new endeavours[20]. This will likely help companies innovate and diversify the space related services, such as providing ground-based systems or satellite-based services, they can offer.

Recommendations

India has done well to ramp up its space science program over the last few years. However, it has nonetheless lagged behind China and the US considerably who have been running successful and proactive space programs in the public and private sectors for decades now. It also lacks in ensuring the presence of a diverse and adaptable space-based arsenal. Understandably, this will take time and resources over and above what is being currently put in if India wishes to match pace with its neighbour. To stay ahead of the curve simply increasing testing is not enough. India must refine its current capabilities and focus energy on accounting for existing gaps in capabilities in India's space arsenal and logistical operations. The nature of testing must also be widened to allow for greater diversity in not only new types of weapons but also new launch capacity. These, as will be elaborated below, will allow for a more well-rounded space agenda for India's military affairs and create the means to achieve it.

Capacity development must happen in several senses. On a technical note, India's existing assets for space warfare are lacking. For instance, today India is only capable of launching its satellites from a limited land-based launch facility. Bommakanti states that adding sea and air-based launching would add to its launch capabilities and create "flexibility and redundancy"[21]. India must also continue to develop co-orbital ASAT technologies that many of its contemporaries possess. In addition to this, newer type of satellite launch modules will allow heavier satellites to be launched. This gives future R&D efforts more room to play with. Finally, on a doctrinal note the Defence Space Agency must not only lay out its vision for the Indian military's role and presence in outer space, it must also lay out where space warfare lands within India's efforts towards conventional, cyber, information, electronic, and psychological warfare and what some points of convergence are.

A potent concern internationally about the militarization of space has been the effect it has on outer space and in earth environment. As a member of the international community, India must heed these concerns and attempt to factor them into its space strategies. These fears stem from, among other factors, the nature of many satellite and weapons systems related testing and the proliferation of space assets more generally as well. For instance, ASAT testing, being an anti-satellite weapon, requires the destruction of an existing satellite already in orbit to demonstrate the missile's viability. Multiple ASAT tests have been conducted since the inception of the technology spurring the amount of space debris generated from the missiles and satellites to increase. The "Graveyard Orbit", as it is often called, now houses many defunct and old satellites that also contribute to space garbage within Low Earth Orbit (LEO) where it can potentially collide with other equipment or manned space crafts[22]. It is thus in India's own interests to develop technologies that simultaneously add value to its defence architecture while tending to concern around the creation of excessive "space junk".

One way to achieve both of these goals is developing non-kinetic space weapons. Non kinetic weapons, which have been described above, are simultaneously potent and produce less debris making them the ideal choice for the environmental dilemmas. Currently India's engagement with the research and development of laser or microwave centric weapons lags behind China's. While China has made significant progress in the development of laser weapons, India's efforts are still at their very earliest stages[23]. Having a diverse range of space enabled arms will add to India's attempts to balance Chinese progress in the space sector. It will also contribute to creating a broad range of warfare capabilities that will work in tandem with emerging cyber warfare and conventional warfare capabilities. Other earth-based means can be the use of electronic warfare to disrupt activities of space-based satellites or the development of non-debris generating ASAT weapons.

All of these alternatives however share one theme, the need for greater attention towards research and development funding for the same. While the DRDO's budget has steadily increased over the past few years, it remains a fraction of the defence budget. It is quite inadequate for the scale of the present R&D necessities which requires the development of cyber, space, psychological warfare tools, while finding indigenous solutions to military modernization needs. This reality only further reinforces the need to involve the private sector further to spur innovation and reduce the burden on government agencies.

ISRO must also be consistently given enough resources and manpower to support such a function. Statements that ISRO might have spread itself too thin, planning for a manned mission to space and a mission to mars, are frequent but the organization is confident that ISRO is doing well with the current workload[24]. However, this does not mean that this will be the status quo as the organization is currently handling both military and non-military projects and is also coordinating private sector engagements through some of its subsidiaries. With the creation of a Defence Space Agency, it is likely that new projects will be initiated as well. India must also work with ISRO to diversify weapons types. All of this will require ISRO to not only gain greater funding and more talent, but also develop a deeper public-private network.

While Antrix was an important first step in ensuring ISRO's access to the private sector, today it is faced with a range of issues that are limiting the development of the private sector. There is extensive demand in the private sector for satellites for commercial use, that is for use by cable tv or by satellite TV operators like TataSky, which ISRO has been unable to consistently cater to[25]. Bureaucracy within Antrix due to regulatory setbacks, such as price regulation, service-level license regulation, etc., required to allow commercial firms access to satellites, is one reason that commercial enterprises may be unable to gain access to satellites at the desired pace[26]. Thus, two key issues crop up, those of de-regulation in the appropriate space and the revamping of public private collaboration mechanisms.

In addition to opening up ISRO facilities to private developers which was stated earlier, streamlining parts production, which is often done by private entities, will help the space program significantly. The Kerala Space Park is a step in this direction and will likely allow for innovation in the field as well. It is equally important to encourage private enterprises to expand beyond part development and expand to the manufacturing or satellites, ground based systems, etc., under the guidance of ISRO. In these cases, ISRO must function as an incubator and facilitator for which the existing bureaucracy and regulatory mechanisms pose as challenges.

Notes

1. Press Trust of India. (2018, April 04). India ranks 3rfd among nations facing most cyber threats: Symantec. Retrieved from The Economic Times: https://economictimes.indiatimes.com/tech/internet/india-ranks-3rd-among-nations-facing-most-cyber-threats-symantec/articleshow/63616106.cms?from=mdr
2. Mohan, P. (2020, October). Cyber Security in India's Nuclear Systems. ORF Issue Brief No. 412. Retrieved from The Observer Research Foundation: https://www.orfonline.org/research/ensuring-cyber-security-in-indias-nuclear-systems/#_ftn6
3. Mohan, P. (2020, October). Cyber Security in India's Nuclear Systems. ORF Issue Brief No. 412. Retrieved from The Observer Research Foundation: https://www.orfonline.org/research/ensuring-cyber-security-in-indias-nuclear-systems/#_ftn6
4. Integrated Defense Staff. (2017, April). Joint Doctrine Indian Armed Forces. Retrieved from: https://bharatshakti.in/wp-content/uploads/2015/09/Joint_Doctrine_Indian_Armed_Forces.pdf
5. Dutta, A. N. (2019, November 25). Indian Army faced two cyberattack attempts every month in 2019. Retrieved from The Print: https://theprint.in/defence/indian-army-faced-two-cyberattack-attempts-every-month-in-2019/325008/
6. Das, S. (2020, September 29). Cyber Warfare: China is Helping Pakistan Hackers Launch Cyber Attacks on India. Retrieved from News 18: https://www.news18.com/news/tech/cyber-warfare-china-is-helping-pakistani-hackers-launch-cyber-attacks-on-india-2916023.html
7. Indian Army. (2018, November 27). Land Warfare Doctrine – 2018. Retrieved from the Indian Army: https://www.indianarmy.nic.in/Site/FormTemplete/frmTempSimple.aspx?MnId=1Z9Go9DN+Be5KsrR5RDXCw==&ParentID=PqvSK9gXBSpj2i2khbJYhQ==
8. Bommakanti, K. (2019, July). Electronic and Cyber Warfare: A Comparative Analysis of the PLA and the Indian Army. Retrieved from the Observer Research Foundation: https://www.orfonline.org/wp-content/uploads/2019/07/OP203.pdf
9. Bommakanti, K. (2019, July). Electronic and Cyber Warfare: A Comparative Analysis of the PLA and the Indian Army. Retrieved from the Observer Research Foundation: https://www.orfonline.org/wp-content/uploads/2019/07/OP203.pdf
10. Ibid.
11. AMCHAM India, FTI Consulting. (2020, April). A White Paper on India's National Cybersecurity Strategy 2020. Retrieved from AMCHAM India: https://www.amchamindia.com/wp-content/uploads/2020/04/AMCHAM_FTI_Whitepaper_Cybersecurity.pdf
12. Integrated Defense Staff. (2017, April). Joint Doctrine Indian Armed Forces. Retrieved from: https://bharatshakti.in/wp-content/uploads/2015/09/Joint_Doctrine_Indian_Armed_Forces.pdf
13. Harrison, T., et. All. (2020, March). Space Threat Assessment 2020. Retrieved from Centre for Strategic and International Studies: https://aerospace.csis.org/wp-content/uploads/2020/03/Harrison_SpaceThreatAssessment20_WEB_FINAL-min.pdf

14. Integrated Defense Staff. (2017, April). Joint Doctrine Indian Armed Forces. Retrieved from: https://bharatshakti.in/wp-content/uploads/2015/09/Joint_Doctrine_Indian_Armed_Forces.pdf
15. Bommakanti, K. (2019, November 15). 'Soft Kill' or 'Hard Kill'? The Requirements for India's space and counter-space capabilities. Retrieved from the Observer Research Foundation: https://www.orfonline.org/research/soft-kill-or-hard-kill-the-requirements-for-indias-space-and-counter-space-capabilities-57832/
16. Harrison, T., et. All. (2020, March). Space Threat Assessment 2020. Retrieved from Centre for Strategic and International Studies: https://aerospace.csis.org/wp-content/uploads/2020/03/Harrison_SpaceThreatAssessment20_WEB_FINAL-min.pdf
17. Asia News International. (2019, June 11). Centre approves new space research agency; DSRA will be tasked with created space warfare weapon systems. Retrieved from First Post: https://www.firstpost.com/india/centre-approves-new-space-research-agency-body-to-be-tasked-with-creating-space-warfare-weapon-systems-6794071.html
18. Kaul, S. (2017, March 17). Need for space governance for India and global space governance. The Journal of Space Safety Engineering. 4(1). Retrieved from: http://www.iffaadindia.org/downloard/Need%20for%20space%20governance%20for%20India%20and%20global%20space%20governance%20%E2%80%94%20ScienceDirect.pdf
19. Financial Express Online. (2020, June 26). India opens space sector to private players: What it means for ISRO. Retrieved from The Financial Express: https://www.financialexpress.com/lifestyle/science/india-opens-space-sector-to-private-players-what-it-means-for-isro/2005105/
20. Ibid.
21. Bommakanti, K. (2019, November 15). 'Soft Kill' or 'Hard Kill'? The Requirements for India's space and counter-space capabilities. Retrieved from the Observer Research Foundation: https://www.orfonline.org/research/soft-kill-or-hard-kill-the-requirements-for-indias-space-and-counter-space-capabilities-57832/
22. Union of Concerned Scientists. (2007, July 21). Debris in Brief – Space Debris from Anti-Satellite Weapons. Retrieved from the Union of Concerned Scientists: https://www.ucsusa.org/resources/space-debris-anti-satellite-weapons
23. Bommakanti, K. (2019, November 15). 'Soft Kill' or 'Hard Kill'? The Requirements for India's space and counter-space capabilities. Retrieved from the Observer Research Foundation: https://www.orfonline.org/research/soft-kill-or-hard-kill-the-requirements-for-indias-space-and-counter-space-capabilities-57832/
24. IANS. (2013, November 5). 'ISRO not spreading thin with different mission'. Retrieved from Business Standard: https://www.business-standard.com/article/news-ians/isro-not-spreading-thin-with-different-missions-113110500825_1.html
25. Kaul, S. (2017, March 17). Need for space governance for India and global space governance. The Journal of Space Safety Engineering. 4(1). Retrieved from: http://www.iffaadindia.org/downloard/Need%20for%20space%20governance%20for%20India%20and%20global%20space%20governance%20%E2%80%94%20ScienceDirect.pdf
26. Ibid.

9

Psychological Warfare

Psychological warfare provides a very different set of difficulties for India than any of the other new fronts of war, such as cyber warfare or space warfare, do. Psychological warfare involves the use of information, such as propaganda, or other non-combat psychological tactics to manipulate information, emotions, strategies, and actions of governments. Psychological operations, or PsyOps, are an essential tool in any military's arsenal that relies heavily on the generation and use of information. The current era, where information is in the plenty and elements of information warfare are already in place through cyber warfare efforts, psychological warfare presents an important dimension that must be harnessed. India's strategic environment, being bordered by China and Pakistan, further underlines the necessity of a strong psychological warfare strategy.

Psychological Warfare as a Tool Against India

Given that psychological warfare aims to build alternative narratives through the use of information, it can be a particularly potent tool to exploit political and social divides within India by regional rivals like China and Pakistan. Relative to China and Pakistan, India lags in generating its own PsyOps and defend against their tactics as well. Pakistan regularly and systematically employs the Chinese concept of the "Three Warfares" by including psychological operations, media manipulation, and legal warfare as a part of its hybrid warfare strategy. The 2020 Pakistani Army Green Book cites these strategies as being central to it's plans to conduct information warfare in Jammu and Kashmir[1]. While India's rhetorical support for information and psychological warfare and its practice are in dissonance, Pakistan's information warfare agencies, such as the Inter-Service Public Relations Wing that handles the military's media presence, are a relatively well-oiled affair. China's integration of information and psychological warfare goes a step further even. China's information warfare tactics focus on "dismantling the adversary's system of systems, with decapitation and paralysis rather than outright destruction" as a part of China's larger focus on "winning without fighting"[2]. Thus, information warfare can be thought of as being at the vanguard of the PLA's efforts to destabilize adversaries even before Chinese troops step in.

Areas such as Jammu and Kashmir and the Indian northeast continue to be vulnerable to Chinese and Pakistani influence. For example, after the Balakot Airstrikes Pakistan immediately exploited the time between the strikes and India's official statement to generate false information through social media that distracted individuals from India's focus on Pakistan's role in Pulwama and its record of sheltering terrorists[3]. In Doklam, reports state that China was working to edge on internal dissent against India's aggressive position during the standoff by claiming that Indian statements are inaccurate and false"[4]. In the Indian Northeast, Chinese influence has been more visible than Pakistani influence. In addition to conducting psychological warfare in Arunachal Pradesh, China has produced propaganda and tried to disseminate alternate narratives regarding the Northeast and its people. One blog article written on Baidu is titled "There is an independent 'little China' in India. They call themselves Chinese and the army is named People's Liberation Army". Here the article is referring to the Northeastern state of Manipur.[5] Such pieces can act as tools of information and psychological warfare, with this peace accessible to Chinese citizens through Baidu.

In the context of the northeast, it is important that the influence of China is not overstated. China is certainly a known supporter of insurgent groups in the region and has given shelter to leaders like Paresh Baruah and funnelled in arms and ammunition. Yet, China's overall influence in the region remains limited. India must be more mindful of the threat propaganda and misinformation local actors can generate in the northeast. Outfits are increasingly turning to social media to not only connect with members and supporters, but also for exploitation and propaganda purposes. Groups have taken to pushing misinformation on social media sites around the time of clashes with the Indian army, at times falsely claiming victory against them[6]. The risk of misinformation doesn't stop there. Social media has also become an important source for projecting propaganda which has even more serious political and social consequences. Propaganda, for example, can be used as a recruitment tool for groups to add members to their cadre. In these cases, disinformation campaigns not only require counter campaigns but also anti-radicalization initiatives with them. The army has been pursuing this with potential ULFA recruits by tracking the activities of known ULFA members who use social media to post content sympathetic to the group and encouraging mobilization for them.[7]

India's PsyOps Capabilities

Given the real danger psychological warfare poses to India's national security, PsyOps must form an integral component of India's warfare strategy that performs in conjunction with cyber and electronic warfare elements. The need for a thorough and involved psychological warfare strategy and mechanisms is growing day by day as concerns about "fake news" grow. Pakistan and China's use of psychological warfare and information warfare, as was highlighted above, is both systematic and well located among larger strategies of hybrid warfare. In this sense India is still quite lacking. As is the case with Cyber Warfare as well, India's psychological warfare efforts are not supported by a strong central doctrine to give it direction nor is it implemented in a robust fashion. All three branches of the armed forces continue to be otherwise hefty structures that are slow to adapt to the social media and digital age, some slower than others. Yet, while psychological warfare cannot perform is a silo, any warfare strategy is incomplete without it in the information era.

Psychological warfare is a consistent element in many of the armed force's strategic documents. The 2017 joint doctrine also situates psychological warfare as a key component of a new generation of war[8]. The Army's 2018 Land Warfare Doctrine states that the Indian Army "shall graduate to a state where mass media shall become an organic part of part of future operations"[9]. The 2012 air force doctrine states that psychological operations are a part of the force's efforts to weaken the enemy's will to fight and can involve the use of offensive air power as well[10]. Finally, the navy's 2015 doctrine states that use of media can be critical for PsyOps, however one must balance "the imperatives of security" and the "benefits of factual reporting"[11]. In each of these cases there is little methodological information on how the services would operationalize these broad acknowledgements of the importance of Psychological Operations. Much like the case with cyber warfare or electronic warfare, broad and general outlines are drawn about the benefits of psychological warfare in the modern world, yet there is no comprehensive document outlining India's approach to instrumentalizing it on an individual service level and cohesively at a national level.

To the tri-force's credit, there have been some changes that have allowed the army, navy, and the air force to better connect with people. The navy has been the most active in this aspect and sets an example for the other forces by being quite active through its social media accounts. Social media has become a tool for information warfare as the Navy has been using it to send constant updates on its operations in its various fields of operation. It sends out the message that the Indian Navy has a strong and reliable presence in the Indian

Ocean and beyond and serves as both a confidence booster domestically and a reminder to the PLAN of its ever-vigilant forces. In 2018 the army also stated that it would reconstitute its media policy given the 21st century communication boom[12]. These steps in the right direction must be replicated in a consistent fashion across the forces so as to not create discrepancies in rules and regulations.

India's use of information warfare in politically sensitive areas should be proactive but sensitive to the sentiments of the space. Consolidating sovereignty in conflicted areas requires that India employ both an armed presence and a "softer" presence that can be crafted through PsyOps and information warfare that helps break down the false claims of the opposing forces. Additionally, an overly force oriented approach can alienate locals and instead make them more susceptible to insurgent propaganda. Thus, India's use of information is of great importance in areas of low intensity conflict in parts of the Indian northeast to create a counter narrative and create a bond between the government and the people.

Recommendations

Steps to create an active and approachable social media presence for the defence forces and agencies is a must in today's day and age. There are a range of social networking services that have varying set-ups and target audiences that can be capitalized upon. However, attracting consistent engagement on Facebook, twitter, or streaming platforms like YouTube can be a challenge. Before one can begin considering social media strategy, establishing presence at the institutional and individual level is incredibly important. While the Navy and the Army operate social media pages consistently the organizations' wider social media policy is directed more towards fears of data security and risk aversion. This is understandable considering that the forces have experienced cases where information has leaked through social media or messaging services[13]. For this reason, there exist considerable rules and regulations for the use of social media on an organizational level while individual soldiers are often banned from using a whole host of internet-based services, including social media and ecommerce sites. The triforces' hesitation to open up such channels risks creating an opaque front between the armed forces, news media and people.

It is also important to consider social media's role as a tool for information warfare. As highlighted above both national and international elements have taken to using social media to promote their cause. In order to effectively combat this India must first be in a position to effectively do so as well. Unlike the UK which has created a new brigade of social media warriors who are tasked with utilizing information warfare and psychological warfare[14], India doesn't have a structure that can do this. In a 2018 statement Army Chief General Bipin Rawat mentioned that Social Media can become a tool to combat proxy warfare which highlights that the army has indeed taken cognizance of this[15]. In a time when information is as valuable as oil or gold, India cannot afford to not capitalize on this resource. General Rawat also stated the army must also invest in adequately educating its cadre on responsible social media use rather than shutting down the possibility of social media use entirely[16].

Part of these initiatives will be to lay out an updated media policy for the three services. The aim should not only be to rethink the Indian military's social media presence and its approach to content generation, but also towards straightening out how to better use traditional media. These reconsiderations must also ensure that the army, navy, and air force's media policies work well with each other rather than functioning in isolation. Any such document must also highlight the importance of information and psychological warfare and elaborate how the military hopes to capitalize on media sources to strengthen India's psychological warfare abilities.

The need for doctrinal clarification is potent in the field of psychological warfare as it is in other emerging forms of warfare. The urgent need to combat psychological warfare emerging in the domestic and international spheres is increasingly taking centre stage as using and distributing propaganda in the digital age is easier than ever before. A detailed psychological warfare doctrine should include information on India's understanding of the term "psychological warfare", what it considers to be tools within the realm of psychological warfare, what mechanisms of psychological warfare it currently possesses and how they are being utilized, as well as address cross-forces collaboration on the use of psychological warfare. Of course, any such attempt must also outline where India wishes to position itself with regards to psychological warfare in both the short term and the long term.

Short term or long-term plans will nonetheless require that India start to consider psychological warfare not as an individual emerging form of warfare but as a part of a larger whole, that is information warfare. Information warfare banks on the synchronized use of cyberwarfare, electronic warfare, and psychological warfare to form a multidimensional front against the emerging national security threats of the 21st century. China's strategic support force is well on its way to doing exactly this. Finally, it is necessary to make sure that suggestions made for future efforts in any doctrine are actionable and achievable. Larger, more complex, efforts towards information warfare require a developed cyber and electronic warfare establishment as well that India lacks. Thus, to spur genuine progress and innovation in the use of psychological warfare, equal progress must be made in other pillars of information warfare.

Notes

1. Pradhan, S. D. (2020, May 08). Pak Army's green book reveals its plans to intensify information warfare in J&K. Retrieved from the Times of India: https://timesofindia.indiatimes.com/blogs/ChanakyaCode/pak-armys-green-book-reveals-its-plans-to-intensify-information-warfare-in-jk/
2. Constello, J., McReynolds, J. (2018, October). China's Strategic Support Force: A Force for a New Era. Centre for the Study of Chinese Military Affairs. Retrieved from the National Defense University: https://ndupress.ndu.edu/Portals/68/Documents/stratperspective/china/china-perspectives_13.pdf
3. Ashok. A. (2020, June). A Battle of Narratives: Challenges of Psychological Warfare of India. Issue Brief No. 235. Centre for Land Warfare Studies.
4. Dasgupta, S. (2017, July 21). Chinese media accuses Sushma Swaraj of lying, putting pressure on its own government. Retrieved from the Times of India: https://timesofindia.indiatimes.com/world/china/chinese-media-accuses-sushma-swaraj-of-lying-puts-pressure-on-its-own-government/articleshow/59703004.cms
5. Thirteen sisters talk about history. (2013, August 17). There is an independent "Little China" in India. They call themselves Chinese and army named the People's Liberation Army. Retrieved from: https://baijiahao.baidu.com/s?id=1575580333451946&wfr=spider&for=pc
6. Anand, M. (2017, October 30). Army to fight N-E rebel on social media. Retrieved from The Asian Age: https://www.asianage.com/india/all-india/301017/army-to-fight-n-e-rebels-on-social-media.html
7. Naqvi, S. (2018, December 10). ULFA using social media to gain foothold in Assam. Retrieved from the Hindustan Times: https://www.hindustantimes.com/india-news/ulfa-using-social-media-to-gain-foothold-in-assam/story-ZyPSBCYcoRLOEQoYlMG9RN.html
8. Integrated Defense Staff. (2017, April). Joint Doctrine Indian Armed Forces. Retrieved from: https://bharatshakti.in/wp-content/uploads/2015/09/Joint_Doctrine_Indian_Armed_Forces.pdf
9. Indian Army. (2018, November 27). Land Warfare Doctrine – 2018. Retrieved from the Indian Army: https://www.indianarmy.nic.in/Site/FormTemplete/frmTempSimple.aspx?MnId=1Z9Go9DN+Be5KsrR5RDXCw==&ParentID=PqvSK9gXBSpj2i2khbJYhQ==
10. Indian Air Force. (2012). Basic Doctrine of the Indian Air Force.
11. Indian Navy. (2012, Updated 2015). Indian Maritime Doctrine. https://www.indiannavy.gov.in/sites/default/files/Indian-Maritime-Doctrine-2009-Updated-12Feb16.pdf
12. Dutta, A. N. (2020, March 6). Army to change 2005 policy to cope with media boom, facebook, twitter, WhatsApp explosion. Retrieved from The Print: https://theprint.in/defence/army-to-change-2005-policy-to-cope-with-media-boom-facebook-twitter-whatsapp-explosion/376445/
13. The Week. (2020, July 09). Indian Army bans 89 apps to prevent sensitive data leaks: Sources. Retrieved from: https://www.theweek.in/news/india/2020/07/09/indian-army-bans-89-apps-to-prevent-sensitive-data-leaks-sources.html
14. Jamadhagni, U., Ramani, R. (2018, May 16). Indian Armed Forces in Social Media: Need of the hour. Retrieved from Indian Defense Review: http://www.indiandefencereview.com/news/indian-armed-forces-in-social-media-need-of-the-hour/

15. Gurung, S. K. (2018, September 04). Social media could be used in combating proxy war: Army Chief. Retrieved from The Economic Times: https://economictimes.indiatimes.com/news/defence/soldiers-should-get-access-to-social-media-within-line-of-control-army-chief/articleshow/65668575.cms?from=mdr
16. Gurung, S. K. (2018, September 04). Social media could be used in combating proxy war: Army Chief. Retrieved from The Economic Times: https://economictimes.indiatimes.com/news/defence/soldiers-should-get-access-to-social-media-within-line-of-control-army-chief/articleshow/65668575.cms?from=mdr

10

Need for Intelligence Reforms

This study has adequately illustrated the ad-hoc nature of defence planning and execution in India. Such ad-hocism extends to the realm of intelligence reform as well. While the country's first intelligence agency, named "Intelligence Bureau" was established in 1887, subsequent developments in India's intelligence agencies have suffered from the downsides of reactionary reform that fails to prepare for the future. As a consequence, most notably the Indian intelligence community was unable to adequately steer response to the 26/11 attack on the Taj Hotel, Mumbai or potentially prevent it. More recently, the build-up of Chinese forces that has led to border clashes has raised questions on the situational awareness of Intelligence agencies and why India was not able to detect and prevent the clashes earlier on.

These instances illustrate that even decades after their establishment, India's intelligence agencies struggle from serious structural deficiencies. In order to establish a defence force that is proactive and not reactive to growing internal and external threats, it is vital that India is able to anticipate threats and take pre-emptive action through its intelligence agencies. This would require structural reform in India's intelligence establishment from the individual agencies' recruitment methods to how the organizations are governed.

While there are a range of reform that can be targeted, here the focus will remain on what are likely the most pressing issues. These include the structure of the Indian intelligence community, poor oversight and accountability across the spectrum of intelligence agencies, avenue for coordination and collaboration between agencies and departments of the government, lack of reform in recruitment practices, slow improvements of technology used by agencies. Some of these areas have been pointed out by larger reviews of India's security sectors, such as the Kargil Review Committee and the 2001 Group of Ministers report. However, government provided self-critique of the Indian intelligence community and recommendations for reform largely remains hidden behind redacted lines within these and other reports. Thus, while a thorough assessment of these issue areas would require a consideration of the government's assessment and reform recommendation relating to them, much of this information remain beyond access. Thus, the first step necessary for a truly holistic consideration of the Indian government's work in the future will require that the government make at least some of those recommendations accessible.

Overview of the Indian Intelligence Community

As highlighted earlier, the Intelligence Bureau was India's first intelligence agency following the establishment of which a range of specialized intelligence agencies have been established within the Indian government. As Dalmia, Datta, and Kapoor highlight the establishment of intelligence agencies in India has often been impromptu, occurring only after a major crisis has already passed.[1] This means that while the range of intelligence agencies within the Indian establishment is not per say unusual, it is important to note that their creation is not situated within any detailed strategic "big picture" plan on how to best structure India's intelligence community. For instance, after its failure to perform well during the 1962 war, the Research and Analysis wing was created as an external intelligence agency aside from the Intelligence Bureau. Similarly, after the Kargil War, the review committee highlighted major deficiencies in intelligence response as a key failure. The result was the creation of two new organizations, the National Technical Resource Organization and the Defence Intelligence Agency which are now criticised for being slow and ineffective[2].

In addition to this, there also exist individual intelligence agencies for the army, navy, and the air force, and intelligence bureaus at the CBI, CID, the revenue department, income tax department, and more. Given the way these organizations often come about, that is as a response to sudden crises, and the lack of a larger national security strategy that can guide the creation and operation of agencies, fears that mandates may overlap and create competition come about as well. Meer collection and processing of intelligence is not adequate of course. Another key part of these agencies' work to report developments to government offices in a timely manner.

Here it is important that relevant information reach bodies like the Cabinet Committee on Security on a regular basis. Chair of the Kargil Review Committee, Mr. K. Subrahmanyam, stated that India still has a long way to go before truly integrating intelligence as a pillar of national security decision making on a regular basis. Unlike the US system where the US president receives daily intelligence briefings, India does not similarly integrate intelligence into its day-to-day security operations at the level of the political leadership[3].

Finally, coordination between the many intelligence agencies poses another major issue. While there have been multiple attempts at creating common nodal agencies for information sharing such as NATGRID and the Multi Agency Centre, they have also been mired by issues. For instance, NATGRID is stated to falter due to the lack of a leader that can rally organizations into efficient crisis response. This has led to the absence of a central intelligence pool for central and state level bodies to access intelligence from reliably. This will unsurprisingly effect India's counter-insurgency and counter-terrorism efforts into the future as well.

Strengthening India's Intelligence Agencies

The cases of the November 26th attacks and the recent India-China clashes show systematic issues with collection of intelligence and its conveyance continue to hamper India's ability to prevent national security threats from taking form. These issues are partly created by poor management and governance reform on the part of the government and individual agencies that have been highlighted above. Yet arguably, the focus has remained on such aspects of reform alone for too long. Equal focus must be given to the fact that the intelligences agencies also contend with a lack of skilled man-power and a lack of key technologies. Intelligence collection and processing is itself a tricky affair and these factors only make it harder for agencies that have to sift through massive amounts of data they receive. For instance, the Takshashila institute's report states that agencies are currently functioning with a 40% staffing deficit[4].

The Intelligence agencies currently rely on recruitment through two channels, the civil services and deputation of existing officers of the IPS, the IAS, and the IFS. This system creates two parallel avenues for recruitment that carry the risk of breeding inefficiencies in the recruitment process according to some[5]. The age of the average new recruit is also quite high with individuals in their late twenties when they are recruited and early thirties if the agency was to wait for them to complete training at their parent service. This means that recruitments happen rather late in the game, in turn reducing the number of years they can of service to the agencies. Recruitment also occurs along two-time frames – short term recruitment and long-term recruitment. Officers can also be sent back to their parent services if their return is requested or if they are deemed a liability to the agency. Arni et. all. state that "this "revolving door" policy, while allowing for flexibility in recruitment, discourages officers from remaining with the agencies for the long term and fully engaging with the organization and developing an attachment to it."[6]

Recruitment in this manner often sees less than ten new officers coming into India's intelligence agencies which has not been enough to address the aforementioned deficit. These officers often do not possess the perquisite area based or language skills to add to the diverse skill set that agencies often require. Teaching recruits in their 30s these skills, particularly language skills, will unsurprisingly be a taller order than teaching those skills to a student in his or her early 20s. Younger talent can be found on university campuses; however, unlike the CIA or other intelligence agencies, Indian agencies do not substantially utilize university deans or former agents working on campuses as talent spotters. India, unlike other countries, also doesn't reply heavily on external consultancies to hire specialized talents to fill in gaps in its own pool of recruits. These measures must be accompanied by relaxation of confidentiality around the nature of intelligence work so as to make joining intelligence agencies appealing to young prospects.

In addition to hiring the best talent, India's intelligence agencies must also be equipped with the best technologies available. Here, as with other areas of procurement, there is a reliance on using externally procured equipment. In the area of intelligence however, this can make India more vulnerable to leaking of confidential information. India's own domestic capacity to develop equivalent or even high-quality variants is limited. This is another space where make in India could have a space to grow as indigenization would provide an added layer of security from external agents. Technological upgradation also includes making the previously mentioned intelligence sharing platforms like MAC and the NATGRID an active part of the intelligence architecture that will help provide vital information to state or substate level agencies where intelligence collection and processing abilities may not be as thorough.

Accountability and Oversight

Krishnaswamy highlights that committees put in place after the 1962 war and the Kargil war consistently highlighted issues with "insufficient intelligence, analysis of available intelligence inputs, timely sharing of intelligence and corresponding follow-up by security forces"[7]. Today, India continues to struggle with these issues. This points to critical flaws in the government's ability to not only point out but also implement reforms over time. Thus, it is important to consider why these issues continue to occur over extended periods of time.

While the government has taken institutional level reform measures to support the creation of a more efficient intelligence force, there have been few efforts to create methods for oversight. Currently, there is no single point organization that monitors the functioning of India's intelligence agencies, reviews their performance, and provides the authority and impetus to jump start reform. Instead, one report points out that the central issue with intelligence agencies has been a "lack of focus and direction, turf-battles, poor coordination, uncorroborated reports"[8]. These issues might be mitigated by the presence of an overseeing authority that is able to clearly delineate the task of each organization. Political oversight by parliamentary institutions provides an added layer of democratic checks and balances over government institutions and can provide a clearer view of the failures of the intelligence community.

Recommendations

Intelligence reform must happen at several levels, from the level of individual recruitment and training to the level of institutional reform and oversight. However, given the nature of the intelligence community which operates under a shroud of secrecy and shares information only on a strict need to know basis, intelligence reform is unlikely to experience the speedy execution it needs. While reform has been mentioned after key events like the Kargil war and the 26/11 case and intelligence oversight has been brought up in the parliament oversight has been brought up in parliament, little has been achieved on these fronts. Rather than focus on the details, the response of the Indian government has more often been to create all new institutions. While this may deal with some gaps left by the mandate of existing agencies, it does not deal with a range of other issues. Instead, new agencies may become just another agency that is mired by the same structural issues that are already present in other agencies.

Reform is most urgent in the areas mentioned in this section. However, before embarking on detailed reform it is important to note that naming and blaming the intelligence agencies for being infective or overly opaque is not the solution. Instead, solutions must be based on an understanding of the inherent difficulties of gathering information and processing it into actionable intelligence. Much of the data that agencies gain access to is often unintelligible or unactionable[9]. To this end, measures must be taken to better train and prepare skilled analysts who are knowledgeable in a range of languages and have their own set expertise.

Thus, rather than relying on the civil services, a range of other sources, including universities, must be utilized to add to the pool of intelligence workers as they often house some of the brightest young minds available. To this end, Indian agencies must remove some of the air of secrecy and mystique around the work of agencies to make them an appealing place of work. Agencies must also build connections with university authorities that will be able to identify potential talents which can be developed into successful agents. To support such efforts, agencies must also lay out their exact requirements from recruits more clearly and emphasize lingual abilities and other relevant skills.

India must also take a thorough look at how much and what aspects of the technology it uses for intelligence operations are indigenously made versus externally procured. Such an assessment must be followed by an account of what equipment is most urgently needed and if India possesses the technical knowhow and the ability to produce it. India can also collaborate with its strategic partners to learn from best practices wherever possible. Developing the technical knowhow in the government or the private sectors will also allow India to be competitive internationally. With private companies increasingly engaging with producing technology for espionage or providing specialized information, the sector, though requiring regulation, has been a major beneficiary of rising demand for such technologies[10]. These companies in turn contribute to strengthening the domestic economy as well. India should also reap the benefits of this demand while strengthening the ability to produce and source indigenously.

Finally, oversight must not be seen as a challenge to secrecy and the "need to know" principle. Instead, relevant parties must be brought into consultation to find a middle way to ensure that adequate oversight, as should be present in any democracy, is achieved while allowing intelligence agencies room to function smoothly. Effort must be poured into re-examining why nodal intelligence coordination organizations like Multiple Agency Coordination (MAC) and NATGRID have failed to function efficiently or start operations to begin with. The function they are meant to serve, which is to ensure that necessary intelligence is available at various levels of government organization to facilitate counter-terrorism and counter-insurgency, are very important given rising tensions with India's neighbours. Thus, it is important that they be brought online as soon as possible rather than postponing their start dates once more.

Furthermore, a major structural problem in intelligence reform has been that executive officers have been kept at lower ranks than their ministerial counterparts and the promotional avenues are limited. There are also allegations of nepotism at various levels within the institution, and very high attrition rates. Many former intelligence employees have joined consultancy firms, market research and risk analysis companies. The training which has been imparted to them at the cost of government exchequer is put into practice in different market research, a fact that requires reviewing.

The intelligence agencies have a strict evaluation and scanning criteria with highly talented individuals joining the force, in the lure of doing something for the country. Yet, bureaucratic process, highly transferable jobs, and the problem of perceived gathering of intelligence as a police act, is equally hampering new talented agents to rise high in the ranks. It is highly unlikely that individuals who have joined an intelligence agency at an early age would ever get to the post of DIG. This technically means that promotions get rare and much more spaced out.

The recruitment process needs to be intense but also not bureaucratically structured. If one investigates the life of a much-celebrated spy who went on to become major in Pakistani army; he was recruited from the ground. Such facilities and approach need to be reinvented. Also, the possibility of long-term covert operations and cover jobs need to be promoted. As the field and the acts of terrorism and espionage have become more specialised and sophisticated, intelligence agencies also have to put boots on ground in a very innocuous way.

It is not that everything about India's intelligence agencies is placed wrongly. Instead to better aid the needs of an internationally rising India, there must be new processes that replace the existing archaic intelligence practices that have become prisoners of history. Many intelligence officials within India work based on policing methods leading to exposure of agents and at times scrupulous planting of stories (passed on as critical intelligence) by anti-national elements.

The intelligence agencies do not have any redressal mechanism which leads to structured corruption and squandering away of public exchequer money on unnecessary expenses. This must be countered through internal auditing and clear accountability. Developing sources and conducting covert operations require careful planning and support systems. At times an intelligence operative feels disappointed because the bureaucratic methods do not allow for incurring expenses which are purely based on rank of an agent.

The inter-agency coordination has also been hampered, because in most of the times the two intelligence agencies of India-IB and R&AW are manned by people from the police services who at times have felt the need to operate in separation from each other and other agencies, leading to a lapse in cooperation. In addition to such facilitation though, the two agencies also need a complete cadre-based promotion system and must develop specialisations in areas such as equity markets, economics and AI as well as cyber security. Finally, premier intelligence agencies in India do not have research divisions, which is strange given the fact that in order to train new recruits the agencies must have a structured curriculum, detailed case studies and in field training which have been till date archaic, to say the least.

Notes

1. Dalmia, et., All. (2020, December 9). India's Enduring Challenge of Intelligence Reforms. Retrieved from the Observer Research Foundation: https://www.orfonline.org/research/indias-enduring-challenge-of-intelligence-reforms/
2. Ibid.
3. Subrahmanyam, K. (2009). Report of the Kargil Review Committee: An Appraisal. Centre for Land Warfare Studies. Retrieved from The Hindu: https://www.thehindu.

com/thread/article16923998.ece/BINARY/Kargil%20Review%20Committee%20 report%20CJ%20SSummer%202009.pdf

4. Arni, et. All. (2019, January). India's External Intelligence Agency: Managing the Human Resource Challenge. Retrieved from Takshashila Institutions:https://takshashila.org.in/wp-content/uploads/2019/01/TDD-Managing-the-HR-Challenge-AA-SM-PK-2019-New.pdf
5. Mehta, S. (2019, April 16). RAW needs to become more like CIA, and move away from IAD & IPS. Retrieved from The Print: https://theprint.in/opinion/raw-needs-to-become-more-like-cia-and-move-away-from-ias-ips/221900/
6. Arni, et. All. (2019, January). India's External Intelligence Agency: Managing the Human Resource Challenge. Retrieved from Takshashila Institutions:https://takshashila.org.in/wp-content/uploads/2019/01/TDD-Managing-the-HR-Challenge-AA-SM-PK-2019-New.pdf
7. Krishnaswamy, J., (2013). Why Intelligence Fails. Retrieved from The Hindu Centre for Public Policy: https://www.thehinducentre.com/multimedia/archive/01611/Why_Intelligence_F_1611665a.pdf
8. Ibid.
9. Ibid.
10. Hopkins, N. & Taylor, M. (2013, November). Private firms selling mass surveillance systems around the world, documents show. Retrieved from The Guardian: https://www.theguardian.com/world/2013/nov/18/private-firms-mass-surveillance-technologies

11

Using Futuristic Strategies

Scholars have long been opinionated that India was desperately in need of its own modernization, and indigenous development for security needs. India is poised at a better position now than ever before, at handling conventional threats, including terrorism. However, technology is changing the nature of the threats, as well as the means through which these threats can be countered. New technologies, like ICT, AI etc, grant opportunities of development and exploitation to states and other non-state actors and groups as well. Countries are on a race to develop AI, Machine learning, Deep learning and other technologies not only for defence but other purposes as well. India must therefore also follow suit in prioritising the development and research of these technologies.

New and Emerging Strategic Technologies - NEST

The Indian government has recently taken a major step in addressing the above however, with the Ministry of External Affairs instituting a new division known as New and Emerging Strategic Technologies (NEST). The institution of the NEST essentially underscores the importance of emerging technologies and the possible threats and challenges they may pose. While a clear mandate of the division has not yet been released by the ministry, a parliamentary reply states that it will deal with foreign policy and legal aspects of new and emerging technologies. The reply goes on to state that "it will enable more active participation of India in global forums in the area of technology governance and promoting our national interests in that context." It is thus believed that NEST will essentially focus on scrutinizing foreign investments and imports that impact the security of the country, while simultaneously seeking to increase international collaboration in facilitating the same.

The creation of the new division essentially follows on the ongoing debates on 5G, which have plagued global forums in recent times. Discussions around the 5G network technologies have given rise to speculation of its usage and the strategic and security risks that it poses. 5G has been posited as the next frontier of the digital revolution, however, with regards to Indian cybersecurity, risks and surveillance have become a significant concern; especially since the Indian government is yet to formulate a robust legal and institution mechanism for the protection of data and piracy. The new division has thus been introduced at a critical time, where assessments may be done in tandem with strategic developments on the international front.

The introduction of NEST during an era of rapid technological development and upgradation can effectively serve and influence India's security in three ways. Firstly, any adoption of newer "strategic" technologies can give impetus to existing processes such as the use and development of artificial intelligence in development and defence sectors. Secondly, emerging technologies can effectively serve to expose India to new vulnerabilities, with rapid development in Artificial Intelligence, and other such technologies. The threats from emerging technologies may emerge in the cyber domain and other domains with risks connected to any procurement of biotechnology, cyber mechanisms and the Internet of Things. India's adoption of a number of systems and mechanisms in its military and offensive capabilities could also seemingly be undermined by exploitation of the very same technologies.

The mandate of NEST must effectively be focused on safeguarding against such threats, on both a tactical and strategic level. Finally, while India has made steps towards ingenious development and procurement of such technologies, much of its needs are dependent on procurement from foreign nations. As appealing as indigenous development of technologies like 5G sound, India is not a key player in technology development and design and is yet to establish an innovative and globally competitive industry which can essentially sustain itself through cooperation across the public and private sectors. In this, all of India's defence and advanced technological procurements must be analysed, so as to maintain its security goals and strategic objectives. Additionally, as has also been noted elsewhere, India's decision on choosing a supplier for the technology can have an immense impact on geopolitics, and even recalibrate the existing balance of power.[1]

Recommendations

India's vulnerability on the technological and cyber front can essentially be used by foreign players to test and operate their dual purpose (i.e. assistive and antagonistic) technologies on its citizens or within its territories. It must therefore meticulously scrutinise the imports and assimilation of emerging technologies into the nation's defence and civilian research and development infrastructure.

Moreover, many systems and technologies that seem relevant today within the defence domain could become redundant within a few years. NEST can essentially ensure that revisions and continuous changes are made to keep with the evolving nature of critical technologies. NEST's analyses and recommendations can be used to comprehensively review imported technologies, build and evaluate domestic technological capabilities, so as to create a robust export and import portfolio of emerging technologies.

NEST must also focus on making command and control systems for strategic systems more robust. Similar to the creation of a complete complex related to software technologies in Bangalore and Hyderabad; for India's security, there is a need for an intricate network involving technical institutions, public-private partnership and commissioning new institutions to work wholeheartedly on the new developing technologies.

In lieu of calls to counter the possibility of drone swarming wars, the DRDO has taken a few initiatives, however, there is a requirement for added emphasis on this front. For symbolic purposes, there is a need for this to be taken up on project basis. Technology cannot be held ransom to bureaucratic inertia and cadre hierarchy. It should be completely free of any bureaucratic intervention. There is also a need for two scientific advisers to the Prime Minister and Defence minister to look into emerging technologies. Many countries in Eastern and Central Europe have the technical capital but do not have funds to support new projects. These can be explored.

The problem with trying to develop new, evolving technologies and areas of research is that the available time frame to achieve results is too short, and in the case of India, which hopes to launch itself into the technology league, it will have to fill in large gaps in its arsenal within this time constraint. This includes supporting the research faculty present in Indian institutions and providing seed money.

One problem with many of the industrial complexes in India is that they look for licensed production and transfer of existing technology from international partners. The NEST is one such field where technology is to be transferred. If the reliance remains on procuring existing technology rather than developing new technology, the tech at hand will always be outdated. Mitigating this requires a better approach on the part of the government that encourages technical superiority by building the human capital of scientists, technicians and professionals.

While advancements in military technology have been great in the west, changes in geopolitics globally mean that new technology is nonetheless needed around the world. It is apparent that friendly countries outside the west are also looking for partners to develop their military capabilities. India, having a sound technology collaboration and science diplomacy initiatives with Singapore, Taiwan and Japan, can look for synergies with these countries.

In any new venture microchips will be critical for developing new technologies. However, India itself does not have a chip fabrication plant as the country lacks a steady electricity supply and there is little desire to build a large chip manufacturing plant in India. India must plan for one to build its chip manufacturing and give impetus to new research.

Further, Digital India and Start up India can be good for initial promotion of innovation and work but there is need for fellowships and for funding study trips for scientists and technicians abroad. The same idea was used by China in the 1990s to get critical technical capital. India can emulate that and build an eco-system which reduces brain drain.

Education is one area and developing thinking and innovating minds is another area to focus on. The New Education Policy is a good initiative but there is a need for incubation modules to be instilled as well. India must identify children with potential and support them throughout their education to bring good minds to contribute to India's progress. Just like commissioning Sainik (military) schools in India, the government needs to work on science schools and technical centres. Even starting new departments in IITs would help in getting the desired talent.

In the UPSC exams a number of students with science backgrounds with excellent track records are deputed to those areas where they lose their skill set and their knowledge becomes redundant. The civil services just like economic services should have technical services boards to look into possibilities of redirecting such talent back into the sciences and developing new vistas for research and development.

Relative to other Asian countries that have also invested in strengthening R&D and developing the scientific minds of the country, data shows that India ranks very low. The few countries which have developed their industries and synergised their R&D programmes are Japan, Korea and Israel. It would be pertinent to initiate collaborative projects to develop technical capital with such partners. AI, machine learning and data sciences are the buzzwords but even in armed forces sparing few officers and giving them training is not enough. There is a need for a separate branch and nurturing new talent.

Indian missions abroad have commercial, trade and cultural counsellors. Similarly, there is an urgent need for technology counsellor to look into various developments that a particular country is making. This is a continuous monitoring process and any per who does not have requisite scientific acumen would not be able to evaluate the research and development done in the focussed area.

Note

1. Tirkey, A. (March, 2020) The NEST: A Pragmatic Addition to India's external Affairs Ministry. ORF. https://www.orfonline.org/expert-speak/the-nest-a-pragmatic-addition-to-indias-external-affairs-ministry-63864/

Conclusion

Within Indian strategic and policy circles, national security is slowly emerging as an essential and pressing issue that requires addressing. Yet, a holistic approach towards such redressal is still in the making. As has been made evident through this book, there are multiple shortcomings within the Indian security establishment that need immediate assessment. The most important of these is the lack of coherence in Indian strategic thought, practice, policy and strategy. Much of the Indian security establishment still functions in an ad-hoc manner, with minimal cross-sectoral collaboration. These is largely due to the fact that in gauging India's security threats and challenges, measures are implemented without complete coherence in approach. India's internal security threats and external security challenges are treated as separate from each other. While this may be justified in lieu of the differing threats that India faces, such an approach essentially neglects the broader political, social and economic context within which specific episodes occur.

In lieu of the immense size and scope of the Indian security establishment, such a goal may seem unachievable, however, what may not be apparent to most is the fact that a certain consensus could possibly be achieved across sectors. As has also been argued elsewhere, India's foreign policy and strategic actions over the past few decades have pointed to a consistency in strategic views and behaviours in spite of the change in governments, ruling parties and circumstances.[1] This consistency is essentially linked to few distinct aspirations that have been prevalent within Indian strategic thought and policy; the first rather operational, while the others, ideational. First, Indian strategic thought has maintained the need to establish India as an entity with strategic autonomy and equality of status within the post-colonial world order. This has been linked to India's other aspirations as well; i.e., the need to ensure domestic sustenance in ensuring India's security, the desire to use dialogue and international law as compared to military means, while simultaneously ensuring national growth and regional influence.

These goals are slowly being realised, as an increased focus is being laid on India's security needs. However, they are yet to be realised in a concrete, shared and coherent manner. The first step in this direction is thus the establishment of a coherent national security strategy that links internal and external threats, and addresses them through both hard and soft mechanisms. This extensive study has essentially outlined each of these in analysis and assessment of India's security establishment; identifying threats to India's internal security and proposing counter measures and strategies; highlighting shortfalls and possibilities in India's defence capabilities and planning; assessing India's strategic environment and navigating a strategy that assures strategic autonomy and finally; assessing non-traditional threats to India's security, while proposing measures to be adopted in the information, cyber and space domains. Through this, this study provides a comprehensive assessment of India's security challenges, showing how progress and success in each sector can be achieved in tandem with others.

Today, as India emerges as a rising power, its security challenges cannot be understood as singular or confined to certain sectors alone. The state essentially must confront multiple and simultaneous challenges, that cannot merely be dealt with through the use of coercive power by the state. Many challenges that characterise India's internal security threats are linked to political, economic or social grievances; all of which must be addressed as well. The vulnerability of India's borderlands today is linked to larger patterns of both crime and geopolitical actions as well. The line between what constitutes an internal threat and what constitutes an external one is also slowly becoming blurred. With covert foreign support to certain insurgent groups in India being uncovered, there is thus a need to revamp India's information and surveillance; possibly in collaboration with its security partners.

Reflecting on such trends, a National Security Strategy for India must therefore adopt a comprehensive approach to domestic, external, economic and ecological challenges; the latter of which have not been emphasized upon within this study, but are nonetheless critical to India's security. The basis for such a strategy must also be the need to highlight inter-linkages and multi-sectoral possibilities in ensuring that a coherent template can be formed; one that run in parallel with both the armed forces and certain ministries in working towards a common goal. Herein, the most critical aspect of this study must be introduced; i.e., India requires a strategy that establishes certain universal long-term goals, which can then be supported and facilitated by cross-sectoral, or sectoral short-term goals.

Securing India's International Aspirations

On the strategic front, India has ensured that while it builds partnerships with countries across its neighbourhood and the world, it has done this while securing its aspirations. Guided by the need to secure its immediate neighbourhood in the Indian Ocean, it has built concretely in partnerships across the board. In this, it has secured partnership with members of the QUAD, countries in Southeast Asia, the Middle East, and with the littoral states of the Indian Ocean. However, some aspects of such security partnerships, such as joint patrols, intelligence monitoring and other engagements can still be built towards with other countries in the region. India's engagement with IOR countries in Africa remains low, while China seeks to build on such partnerships towards its own benefit. This could serve as a significant strategic threat in the future.

Nonetheless, in other sectors India still maintains its course in securing its strategic autonomy and initiating initiatives aimed at establishing itself as a regional security provider, while simultaneously securing the support of countries like the United States, Russia and France. Herein though, while India has secured its strategic autonomy in the short run, with the slow progress of relations with the US, there could be threats of strategic leveraging in India's foreign policy agendas and goals by the US. This possibility must be acknowledged by the Indian government and minimised in due course. Additionally, coherence in India's security strategy in its neighbourhood is premised on the need to outline certain strategic challenges, which it is yet to do; the most important of which is China. In lieu of its assertive behaviour in recent times, the China threat is not likely to subside soon, and India can expect frequent incursions across its borders and within its maritime zones from China. In this, while India has secured the support of the QUAD countries and other adversaries of China, it is yet to clearly outline it as a threat, thus hindering its own operational and strategic capabilities and planning in both the short and long term.

In order for India to develop a clear and coherent strategy across the next few decades, it needs to establish a definitive understanding of the threats in its strategic neighbourhood; at least in the short term. In the longer term, there is a requirement for it to establish a 30-year strategy that positions it as the net security provider in the Indian Ocean. This must include an emphasis on possible logistics sharing agreements with smaller nations, island development policy, influence over multilateral agendas in the IOR and possibilities of further bilateral engagements with countries in the region.

Securing India's Internal Security

India's internal security situation has improved tremendously over the past few decades, with stability being achieved in a number of key regions. However, this area shall remain of paramount importance in the coming years as well. The process of ensuring a country's national security is after all a continuous one which cannot be disregarded. Herein, certain issues still remain that require constant redressal; namely the possibilities of radicalization along with issues in the North East, Jammu and Kashmir, and Left-Wing Affected areas. This study has shown that while dealing with such issues, the government and security establishment must adopt two approaches in parallel with each other; the first aimed at harder security measures in dealing with offenses, while adopting a softer approach in dealing with potential communities that can commit offences. Political upheaval and unrest have often been observed to be linked to socio-economic issues; a fact that needs to be addressed in any national security strategy.

A national security strategy must essentially seek to assess and review certain institutional mechanisms such as the UAPA and NIA that are currently in place; revitalising the use or even restricting the abuse of such mechanisms. Certain national security issues and the security forces in charge of dealing with the same must be monitored through a coherent national mechanism. Along with this, the establishment of additional security mechanisms that can focus on only specific issues must also be initiated; this is especially with reference the Anti-Terror Squads that have proven to be a success in a number of states. On softer approaches, the state must adopt separate approaches to anti-radicalization, de-radicalization and counter-radicalization based on the level of radicalization visible. Such an approach can essentially secure regions that could become potential areas of instability, and a national threat to the country.

Military Modernization

Modernization of India's armed forces is a crucial task that is currently occurring under strict budgetary constraints. The struggle is to pursue the extensive requirements of military modernization within reasonable time frames while abiding by budgetary constraints. Given this, a few broad goals must be pursued in the long term that can help direct the task of military modernization in the short and medium term. These are to clearly determine current and future national security threats, establish doctrines and strategies to support combating these threats, and to reorganize force structure in order to best facilitate the previous two points. In the short-term, focus must be put on supporting the modernization needs of the individual forces, particularly the Indian Air Force. Upgrades and modifications are required on the indigenously developed light combat helicopters and the air force could also use development of its unmanned aerial capacities. Timely acquisition of critical resources is also critical. While the Indian government has helped promote acquisitions a lot, much remains to be done to enable the acquisition of other capital assets. To this end the involvement of the private sectors has been critical. Finally, to support operations on its borders, India must extend greater funding to its 17 corps and work to establish a second Mountain Strike Corp.

Police & Paramilitary Management

Police and the Indian paramilitary form a critical pillar supporting counterinsurgency, peacekeeping, and border guarding functions in the Indian Northeast and the Rust Belt. With multiple forces and ministries working across the region, duties and the chain of command are often muddled. Inter-departmental and inter-organizational conflict often compromises the force's ability to fully carry out its duties. In the northeast the Assam rifles would be better able to conduct counterinsurgency tasks if they are not simultaneously tasked with carrying out border guarding duties. To this end, the MoHA would benefit from placing another existing wing of the CAPF to guard the Indo-Myanmar border. In the rust belt the competition between state and central level organization is compromising cooperation and creating logistical issues. Here, the MoHA must clearly distinguish roles and responsibilities. One solution could be to consider the unification of the various paramilitary forces by the tasks they are meant to perform, helping clarify their individual roles. This could lead to the creation of one branch handling security and law and order operations, while the other handles counter-insurgency operations. Finally, India's paramilitary system must be imbibed with the same strategic culture that thrives around the Indian military through think-tanks like CLAWS, NMF, USI, IDS etc. This will allow for the creation of new knowledge in the field of Indian paramilitary operations that will be critical to informing a new generation of paramilitary operations, leadership, and policies.

Defence Procurement

Procurement remains a cumbersome and ad-hoc process in India that is constrained by a slow bureaucracy, mixed record with R&D and financial constraints. For procurements and acquisition to happen smoothly, India must improve its planning mechanisms in the MoD and in other government ministries, like that Ministry of Finance, that supports these efforts. Funding should be provided in blocks of several years, instead of the budget changing on a yearly basis. This only creates uncertainties in the procurement process as plans are often delayed to compensate for shrinking budgets. In the planning phase, the MoD and the individual services must streamline the process of indigenous development to ensure it's both efficient and timely and produces quality end products. Given the success of the Navy's design department, perhaps it would be better for the individual services to have their own design departments. They could then consult the DRDO and other relevant agencies through the design process. Focus must also be placed on producing parts and other equipment, in addition to big ticket purchases. Here too supporting R&D through funding and private sector involvement can be of benefit.

Integrated Information Networks

Integrated Information Networks require further investment for the long term at the level of individual services and the national level. While each of the three services operate multiple information networks of their own, these need immediate modernization. Not only do networks across the services need updating, but these networks must also be connected to one another to allow for smooth sharing of necessary information across forces. To this end, greater focus must be given to planning out what kind of systems must be acquired to facilitate this and providing the services the funds necessary to make it possible. The services must be consulted to understand the exact nature of the systems and what aspects are in the most urgent need for modernization. However, modernization of information network systems must also be supported by efforts at the level of the CDS, the ministries, and the private sector. Collectively, these bodies should be consulted to create a comprehensive vision of what all the MoD and the services wish to accomplish using integrated information systems and how it would benefit India in terms of securing its national security interests. This should happen at the earliest so as to bolster long term modernization efforts. Finally, the MoD and the Department of Technology must also investigate viable ways to fast track the development of key technology enablers that could enhance integrated information networks. These technologies include the development of indigenous 5G networks and AI enabled systems.

Cyber and Space Security

Cyber and Space security are relatively under-developed sectors within India's defence sphere where much work remains to be done in terms of advancing technology and policy. This will require the participation of actors across levels, from the Ministry of Defence, Ministry of Communication and Information Technology, ISRO, DRDO, and the private sector. Significant attention must be given to the crafting of National Cyber Security Strategy and finalizing the draft National Space Policy by the CDS in consultation with these various stakeholders. Given that procurement of foreign equipment and software can pose risks to security, domestically developed alternatives may prove to be more secure. To this end, India would benefit by continuing to reduce regulations that make private sector participation difficult and providing government agencies with the required funds to be able to carry out new research and development initiatives. Finally, India must make developing cyber warfare capabilities a long-term priority that is built up by supporting strategy and R&D in the short and medium term. Space warfare capabilities must be diversified through the development of new weapons and launch capabilities. This would entail ensuring that weapons are capable of launch from air, sea and land bases and that launch vehicles can carry heavier loads. These are goals for the long term that must be supported by greater financing and recruitment of top-notch talent at ISRO. Newer weapons, such as non-kinetic weapons, and laser and microwave-based weapons, also must be developed. Both cyber and space security/warfare efforts must be considered in the context of larger efforts to build up information warfare capabilities in India.

Psychological Warfare

In the short-term India's three forces must start using social media tactfully to shape public image and promote transparency. While fears of cyber security are valid, the extensive regulations on social media usage and the military's ad hoc interactions with traditional media will prove to be a hurdle in smoothly conducting information warfare. Soldiers must be trained on how to best approach social media use, rather than banning it outright. Perhaps, like the UK, India can benefit from a unit of social media specialists that are tasked with utilizing media platforms to facilitate information warfare and psychological warfare. In the long term, much like other fields, psychological warfare will also benefit from doctrinal clarification on how India envisions its role and how it wishes to pursue psychological warfare in the short and long term. Finally, psychological warfare must not be thought of as an endeavour in and of itself. Instead, psychological warfare must be considered in India's strategy documents as part of information warfare efforts that also encompass cyber warfare and electronic warfare capabilities.

Looking to the Future

As India grows in both economic and strategic power, a national security strategy will become absolutely essential; building towards a common, coherent approach within India's security establishment. Within each sector there is a need to establish a strategy that aids India's rise in global engagement, military prowess and economic growth. Stability is crucial to a country that is poised to become a key focal point in a highly competitive and important geostrategic location. In this, while internal aspects of force projection, counter radicalization and police management are ensured, India must also fashion a strategy that accounts for upcoming trends in this constantly evolving world. The introduction of the NEST is a key development in this regard, however there must also be enhanced progress made on securing India's data privacy, cyber domains and advancement in the space domain.

As warfare and strategic challenges shift from the traditional to the non-traditional, India must be prepared to counter them in full. This must be achieved through international collaboration and internal development as well; through the utilization of strategic assets, leveraging of international partnerships, modernization of India's military, monitoring of internal police and paramilitary forces, and the securing of agendas on the non-traditional front. Clearly outlined progress along these lines will ensure that India's rise as a great power is ensured and smoothly facilitated.

Note

1. Bajpai, Basit and Krishnappa. (2014) Introduction: India's Grand Strategic Thought and Practice *in India's Grand Strategy: History, Theory, Cases.*

The Authors

Dr. Pankaj K Jha is Associate Professor and Associate Dean of Research, as well as the Director for Centre for Security Studies at the Jindal School of International Affairs, O.P Jindal Global University. He was the Director (Research) with the Indian Council of World Affairs for more than two and half years. He also worked as Deputy Director with the National Security Council Secretariat (2012-2013) and was closely associated with the national security apparatus in India.

Mr. Zeus Hans Mendez is student at the Jindal School of International Affairs, Sonipat, and Centre Coordinator at the Centre for Security Studies, JSIA. His research has focused on topics of military modernization, insurgencies, deradicalization within the realm of Security and Strategic Studies with a specific interest in the Indo-Pacific region. He is also focused on understanding conflict resolution, and peacebuilding in active conflict environments. Additionally, he serves as Research Coordinator at the Centre for Middle East Studies and Research Assistant at the Centre for Security and Strategy Studies (CeSCube).

Ms. Swati Lakshmi Batchu is student of Jindal School of International Affairs, Sonipat, specializing in Peace and Conflict Studies and Research Assistant at the Centre for Security Studies. Her research interests include information warfare, space warfare, para-military activity and insurgencies, and area studies. Additionally, she is also invested in studying international peacekeeping and peacebuilding, and systematic violence reduction in conflict areas. She is currently also working as Student Coordinator for the Centre for India-China Studies and Research Assistant for the Centre for Afghanistan studies.

Mr. Rayan V Bhagwagar is student of Jindal School of International Affairs, Sonipat and Research Assistant at the Centre for Security Studies. He is currently pursuing a Master of Art's degree in Diplomacy, Law & Business, specialising in Defence & National Security Studies. His fields of interest lie in modern military history, strategic affairs, tactics, platforms and national security, with a keen eye on Chinese military development and the global initiative toward containing the threat.